MOUNTIES, MOOSE, AND
THE PATTERNS AND CONTEXT OF OUTPORT CRIME

Three different types of 'crime' are examined in this comprehensive study of criminal behaviour and law enforcement in two small Newfoundland fishing villages. The 'crimes' include acts deemed criminal by the rules and regulations of the state but not necessarily by local sentiment, and acts that violate local norms but are not criminalized by the state. The descriptions of criminal activity and community sentiment are based on almost a decade of participant observation. Because the outports are so different from urban, industrial, capitalistic domains typically studied by those interested in crime, the study relates the unique expressions of outport criminal behaviour to patterns of settlement, developments in the fishery, the history of law enforcement, and cultural change.

Norman R. Okihiro looks at crime arising from economic subsistence behaviours – hunting, gathering, and domestic production activities that have long been supported or tolerated in the outports. These include big game poaching and the production and consumption of moonshine. These traditional activities are of particular interest because they have been subject to increasing regulation by the state, a situation that has markedly affected the way participants tailor their behaviour.

Okihiro also looks at such conventional crimes as assault, theft, and domestic violence. The incidence of and behavioural patterns associated with these interpersonal crimes in the outports he finds to be the result of cultural constraints and the effective informal mechanisms of social control found in the outports.

The third type of crime involves exploitative behaviour that stems from the historical and continuing state of economic vulnerability, impoverishment, and powerlessness of most outport residents. He describes the processes and tactics used by fish plant operators, merchants, police, and outside professionals to exploit outport inequalities in power or influence, as well as the structural and cultural bases of continued tolerance of exploitation among the residents themselves.

Okihiro concludes with an examination of the effect of the unprecedented collapse of the inshore fishery and the impact of subsequent government adjustment and conservation policies on the outport way of life, paying special attention to current and likely future patterns of crime and civil disorder, and offers recommendations for enlightened government policies.

NORMAN R. OKIHIRO is Associate Professor of Sociology at Mount Saint Vincent University.

NORMAN R. OKIHIRO

Mounties, Moose, and Moonshine: The Patterns and Context of Outport Crime

UNIVERSITY OF TORONTO PRESS
Toronto Buffalo London

© University of Toronto Press Incorporated 1997
Toronto Buffalo London
Printed in Canada

ISBN 0-8020-0891-7 (cloth)
ISBN 0-8020-7874-5 (paper)

Printed on acid-free paper

Canadian Cataloguing in Publication Data

Okihiro, Norman R. (Norman Ryukichi), 1948–
Mounties, moose, and moonshine

Includes bibliographical references and index.
ISBN 0-8020-0891-7 (bound)
ISBN 0-8020-7874-5 (pbk.)

1. Rural crimes – Newfoundland.   2. Rural crimes –
Newfoundland – Public opinion.   3. Law enforcement –
Newfoundland.   4. Fishing villages – Newfoundland.
5. Newfoundland – Social conditions.   6. Public
opinion – Newfoundland.   I. Title.

HV6809.N5034 1997   364.9718   C96-932378-6

University of Toronto Press acknowledges the financial assistance to its
publishing program of the Canada Council and the Ontario Arts Council.

This book has been published with the help of a grant from the Humanities
and Social Sciences Federation of Canada, using funds provided by the
Social Sciences and Humanities Research Council of Canada.

Contents

Preface

Like many other Canadians and Americans who have met people originally from small villages in Newfoundland, I have noted and occasionally
wondered about some of their ways: a warm and personal interactional
style, helpfulness, a general lack of prejudice, and typically, a strong
attachment to their home province. In the large cities of North America,
these traits are rare and are sometimes seen as maladaptive and inappropriate, a fact which is perhaps best expressed in 'Newfie' jokes, which
generally portray Newfoundlanders as good-natured but unsophisticated,
and therefore easy to take advantage of.

When the opportunity arose to visit an outport in the mid-1980s, I was
curious to observe, first hand, what life was like there. On my first visit,
I could not even make out the jokes that people were telling because of
the unfamiliar accent and idiomatic turns of speech characterizing the
particular village. What did stand out in my mind, however, and could
not be hidden behind linguistic and cultural barriers, were two things.
First, there was an unmistakable vitality, authenticity, and consideration
for others marking face-to-face interaction, including interaction with
relative strangers. It was easy to see where the image of the friendly Newfoundland originated. Secondly, the manner in which people supported
themselves was very different from that in urban areas. Almost every adult
worked, often seasonally, in fishing or forestry-related jobs, but they also
engaged in a whole round of activities, both individual and collective,
which together enabled their families and the community to survive.

Initially, though I became fascinated by these and other facets of
outport culture, I did not think that, in terms of crime, the outports of
Newfoundland were particularly interesting. After all, in the small fishing
villages where almost everyone is a relative or friend, serious conventional

crime is rare. It was on my first winter trip to Newfoundland that my interest in outport crime was piqued. In winter, a large percentage of men became preoccupied with the hunting of moose. While the same excitement that urban recreational hunters undoubtedly feel about going into the woods and bagging a large animal was obvious among the outport people I knew, there was an important difference as well. The cultural orientation was distinctive. Hunting a moose here was more than just a desirable leisure pastime. For some men, the hunt was the central seasonal focus of their lives, providing purpose and animation to their activities. Indeed, the hunting was important economically and supported culturally, so much so that some local men were willing to hunt even without a licence, despite increasingly severe punishments for getting caught. Many openly admitted they were poachers.

As I became more familiar with outport life, other peculiar and sometimes puzzling facets were revealed. People illegally distilled moonshine and consumed it, but were much more reluctant to do so openly than they were to poach. Rugged people appeared to be inordinately afraid of the Royal Canadian Mounted Police, but not of fishery officers or game wardens. Competent, apparently self-sufficient individuals treated plant owners, merchants, and people who provided professional services to the community with a deference bordering on servility, and they were willing to ignore abuses of power and exploitation that resulted. Fish plant workers drove themselves to work harder despite the fact that, in doing so, they reduced their working hours and pay. Finally, the competitiveness and the lack of effective privacy characterizing the outports generated a lot of tension between people, but rarely resulted in physical attack.

In order to make sense of what was often enigmatic behaviour, I started reading the academic literature on outport life. I began with general anthropological accounts of outport culture, but it quickly became clear that an adequate understanding of outport criminal behaviour required some familiarity with its economic, historical, and social, as well as its cultural, context. Thus, I began a snowball process of reading. This has included information about the unique history and patterns of settlement of Newfoundland's outports, its singular history of government (in particular, the development of law enforcement structures), and, importantly, major economic developments in the Atlantic fishery and their impact on outport life. This book is thus an attempt to provide not only descriptions of the peculiar patterns of outport crime observed through the field work, but also an explanation of the patterns through systematic treatment of the context in which the patterns have developed.

The catastrophic collapse of the ground fish stocks of Newfoundland in 1992 has not only resulted in a complete cessation of commercial fishing for ground fish, which is the backbone of the outport economy, but has also triggered further government restriction on the subsistence activities that have allowed outport residents to weather previous declines in the local economy. Motivated by a conservation ideology, the state has embarked on a series of measures whose intent is to reserve natural resources to a smaller number of individuals and corporations. The first step in the process of disenfranchisement appears to have been a clamping down on the very subsistence activities that have enabled impoverished outport people to survive hard times in the past. At present, more damaging policies have been delayed in Newfoundland by the moratorium and all fishing. However, if current policies in other parts of Atlantic Canada are an indication, government policies and regulations will be enacted to force powerless people out of the fishery.

My hope is that this book will contribute to the development of enlightened policies. What is at stake here is not just another government policy, but the potential destruction of the outport way of life. Most Canadians and Americans know little about life in the outports. With the current preoccupation with cutting government spending and downsizing, there are many who would unthinkingly cut any social program. Blindly pursuing present policy trends will rob outport people of traditional opportunities to support their families and of the chance to remain resourceful and adaptive, and will demoralize them. By pitting individuals with different economic interests against each other, inappropriate policies will help tear apart the social fabric of outport communities.

If the present fishing and hunting policies and enforcement practices continue, we can expect collective confrontations and expressions of frustration against the government such as are already happening in parts of Atlantic Canada and British Columbia. This will engender negative images in the media. By providing a description and analysis of facets of outport culture – an admirable culture based on economic adaptation, hard work, and mutual respect – I hope that his study will not only give readers an appreciation of a different way of life, but will provide support for reasonable policies that will balance the interests of those affected with the broader concerns for balancing the budget. What we need is for enlightened policy makers at the federal and provincial level to reconsider the regulations and policies affecting outport life, before further and irreparable damage is done to a Canadian way of life worth saving.

Acknowledgments

First of all, I would like to acknowledge the organizations which provided funding for me to carry out the research. An extended period of field work was possible because of funding received from the Social Sciences and Humanities Research Council of Canada for my proposal to study 'Perceptions of Policing in a Rural Non-farm Area' (SSHRC General Research Grant #410-86-0817). A SSHRC Sabbatical Leave Fellowship (#451-86-0103) also helped defray the expenses of carting self and family to Newfoundland for several months. Research support for developing the original SSHRC proposal was obtained through a Research Seed Money Grant received from the Atlantic Institute of Criminology, Dalhousie University.

Mount Saint Vincent University has consistently supported my research efforts through the provision of sabbatical research leaves and approvals of funding to present related papers at conferences. In this regard, the Annual Meetings of the Atlantic Association of Sociologists and Anthropologists have proven to be the best forum for feedback from other academics. The Institute of Social and Economic Research, Memorial University of Newfoundland, graciously provided a Leave Fellowship during the early part of the research period. Staff associated with ISER and Memorial University's Centre for Newfoundland Studies also proved that the stereotype of the helpful and friendly Newfoundlander has a basis in reality.

I would like to thank Elliot Leyton in Anthropology and Larry Felt in Sociology at Memorial University; Bob Kaill, the former Director of the Atlantic Institute of Criminology, Dalhousie University, and Donald Clairmont, the present Director; and Mr Virgil Duff, Executive Editor of the University of Toronto Press, for their encouragement.

I wish it were possible to list the names of the individuals who provided information, whether it was informally, in conversation, through formal interviews, or through sharing with me a part of their lives. Obviously, because of the nature of the subject matter, this is not possible. Indeed, because of the need to protect the identity of individuals by obscuring kinship relationships and avoiding detailed personal descriptions, even the participants might not recognize themselves in this study. To these people, nevertheless, I extend a heartfelt thanks not just for providing the grist of this research study, but for the ongoing demonstration of a life style which is not only viable, but, in the face of chronic economic uncertainty, admirable in terms of the way people respect and treat one another. I will mention two individuals who were indispensable to this research. The open-door hospitality and generosity (not to mention cooking ability) of my mother-in-law, Emily Ropson, not only made the visits of our family informative and enjoyable, but facilitated ongoing contact with a veritable stream of her friends, relatives, acquaintances, and even strangers who likewise dropped in and always felt welcome. Willis Loder, the old-timer and keeper of the fire, showed the virtue of outport life through his remarkable memory of people and events dating back to his first day in school, and his ability to 'jump over my head.'

It was through my wife, Doris, that I was introduced to and have gained a real appreciation for outport life. From the start she has provided not only a fountain of the local knowledge that is critical to understanding the intimacies of interpersonal relationships in the outports studied, but has proven to be a concerned and outspoken commentator on the outports in general. I would especially like to thank Doris and our son Michael for interrupting their lives so the winter field work for this research could be pursued, and for the sacrifices they have endured by forgoing other activities in favour of yet another visit to Newfoundland. Needless to say, in the sex-segregated world of the outports, most of the information on female behaviour, attitudes, and perspectives on outport crime and social order was the result of Doris' interaction with other women.

Shortly after embarking on the voyage of discovery that this research has meant, Jonathan was born. He too has had an important role in the how this research project has unfolded. Children form natural bridges of communication between adults by giving them common interests, and not only with other parents, but with a large number of persons in the family-oriented outport society who invariably remember him as a baby or a small boy and still ask about him. I hope that he will grow up to appreciate as I do the wonderful opportunity to live amongst people who, by cultural inclination, treat others as the unique people whose lives matter to them personally.

I dedicate this book to Doris, Michael, and Jonathan and to the informants and respondents in Main Harbour and Fish Arm who must remain nameless.

A view of Fish Arm showing the local topography

A view of part of Main Harbour and Northern Bay

A fisherman's wharf, showing crab pots and small fibreglass boats used in the
inshore fishery

A long liner, typical of those used in the near shore fishery since the mid-1970s

A cabin in the woods. Such cabins are favoured by many outport residents as hunting bases and places to get away to.

Snowmobile towing a komatik, or hand-made sled, often used for towing and protecting heavier loads

A bull moose, felled in the fall

A fleeing moose

Skinning a freshly killed moose, in preparation for quartering

A moonshine still

The author aboard a long liner, breaking up ice from a glacier

MOUNTIES, MOOSE, AND MOONSHINE

1

Introduction

The academic study of crime and crime coverage from the mass media almost exclusively focus on crime committed in modern, urban, industrial or post-industrial milieux. Most Americans and Canadians live in such areas, and this is where the most pressing social issues about crime emanate. Daily we are bombarded with news of the most recent criminal acts almost invariably taking place in an urban conglomeration, and for most of us it is easy to extrapolate from the reported situation to our own. Living in or near largely homogeneous towns or cities, most of us assume that almost everyone else in North America lives in a roughly similar manner.

Academics fare no better than the mass media at differentiating the wider contexts within which crime occurs in North America. Criminologists report on patterns of murder, rape, theft, community reactions, policing, victimization, and so on, typically taking for granted that the social, economic, and political contexts of their studies are of relatively minor importance and certainly not problematic enough to limit the extent to which the patterns they reveal can be generalized. Specialists and experts in one city are regularly consulted about crime in other cities. National markets for experts in criminology exist. The end result is that our knowledge of crime in North America has taken on a universal façade, downplaying consideration of the context in which the studies have taken place, and assuming that general patterns of criminal activity can be and have been discovered.

Occasionally, however, one runs across a situation where the wider context is so completely different from the usual, where the industrial, urban, and democratic assumptions of modern North American life are so profoundly challenged, that a more comprehensive treatment of crime

Map 1
Newfoundland in Relation to North America

is required, one that provides explicit treatment of not only the patterns of crime and reactions to it but also of that wider context. This is the case of the outports on the northeast coast of Newfoundland.

A World of Difference[1]

Newfoundland 'outports' are small fishing villages, thinly spread over the long and inhospitable shoreline of the island of Newfoundland, Canada's most easterly province, which juts far out into the cold waters of the

North Atlantic Ocean and is closer to London than Vancouver or Los Angeles. The world of outport Newfoundland is rural, not urban. But unlike the bulk of rural areas, in which farming is the main activity and there is usually considerable distance between individual homes, people in outports live physically, and socially, close to each other, though each coastal settlement tends to be isolated from others by distance and difficulty of transportation. In urban areas, many everyday activities and interactions occur among relative strangers. As a result, going to a grocery store, driving on a freeway, shopping at a mall, attending school, or going to work are relatively impersonal activities. Given the sheer number of people with whom one can have potential contact, there is always a likelihood that one could be a victim of criminal attack committed by a person or persons unknown.[2] In spite of the fact that the individual likelihood of attack is low, partly because people take precautions to avoid potentially dangerous situations, many feel constantly vulnerable to crime. In contrast, the outports that are studied in this book have total populations in the hundreds, not thousands or millions, and are isolated by geography. Everyone is a familiar, except for occasional strangers who are easily identified and observed. Thus, what crime does occur is almost always intensely personal in nature, involving perpetrators and victims known to each other. Fear of criminal attack by strangers is almost non-existent.

Unlike cities where a diversified industrial and service economy exists, the economic backbone of the outport has always been, and continues to be, the multi-species inshore commercial fishery, composed of individuals and small crews fishing within a few miles of their homes for a number of seafood species as they migrate into the area or their harvest season occurs. Those engaged in the inshore fishery, though nominally independent fishers,[3] have historically been economically dependent on and tied into an exploitive mercantile system whereby, in exchange for fishing and subsistence supplies, they were required to 'sell' sun-dried salted fish prepared privately, through efforts of the whole family, to the local fish buyer at prices set by the buyer. Though there have been significant transformations in the Atlantic fishing industry, notably a shift to fresh and frozen seafood processed in local plants and to the development of new methods and technologies of fishing that compete for the catch with the traditional small-boat inshore segment, from the point of view of most in the outports, the basic situation of dependence on fishing and generally low and unreliable incomes derived from fishing and fish-plant work remains remarkably the same.

In this region, rather than being engaged full-time in a typically narrowly defined job, most men,[4] even those directly involved in the commercial fishery, engage in a myriad of traditional outdoor economic activities, which are necessary to supplement fishing industry incomes and government assistance. These involve hunting and gathering of what are treated as "common property" valuables, things which are not considered as the private property of an individual or individuals. Formal regulations, proscriptions, and rules concerning these activities are noticeably missing compared to the urban situation, resulting in a strong sense of physical freedom in the sparsely populated areas around the outports. Property laws that are taken for granted in more populated regions of capitalist countries are ignored or held in abeyance, or simply not enforced. Cutting trees for firewood or for residential construction purposes (cutting "sticks'), for example, is done routinely by a large proportion of the able-bodied male population, with little regard for who formally retains cutting rights.[5] The sound of chain-saws is a familiar one to most people in the outports any time of the year. Fishing for family consumption has been allowed, until recently, with virtually no restrictions other than those imposed by nature. In winter, snowmobilers intent on cutting wood, hunting, or just going for a ride follow trails that often traverse between houses or on what in urban areas would be considered private property. There is little concern for recognized borders, a situation made all the more common by a dearth of deeds and official titles to property. As a final example, wild berries are picked whenever and wherever they grow, by anyone who cares to do so. The necessity of engaging in economic foraging activities and the community values supporting these traditional pursuits, including the very different perception of property rights, limit the extent to which patterns of urban and industrial crime described elsewhere can be applied to the outports.

Perhaps nowhere is the difference between the rest of urban North America and the outports so great as in the area of political institutions and government. In urban areas, we tend to assume that a reasonably democratic political system has developed and is in place. The history of outport government is certainly the strangest and most peculiar among Western nations, violating the assumption of an ever-increasing democratic orientation. Because of the economic importance of the fishery, a succession of outside fishing interests has effectively governed the outports, starting with the fishing admirals of England's west country fishing enterprises and continuing most recently with the federal government of Canada's Department of Fisheries and Oceans. Local fishermen have had little direct input on issues affecting their livelihoods. Indeed, the enforcement of a growing number of regulations and policies by state fishery and wildlife officers in the past few decades has increasingly affected the life style and the propensity for engaging in illegal behaviour among outport residents. The inability of outport citizens to control much of their economic destiny has its political and national parallel in the fact that, during the 1930s, a bankrupt Newfoundland government voluntarily gave up power in exchange for rule by a Commission of Government from England. In 1949 Newfoundland voted to join Canada as the tenth province.

Beyond the central economic matters in which outside interests have unilaterally determined policy, neglect is probably the best way to describe the relationship between the outports and various levels of government. Unlike urban areas where the government provides basic services that allow the cities to function, the small, scattered outports have received very little in the way of formal government services. The result has been that policing, fire fighting, sewage, recreation, schooling, road building, social services, and most other functions have been provided informally by the outport residents themselves. A tradition of mutual support and co-operation has thus emerged. This is particularly important in the area of crime and social order. Even today, the deployment of police officers is problematic, time-consuming, and expensive. The Royal Canadian Mounted Police, who service the non-urban regions of the province, make only occasional, and quickly noted, appearances the outports, usually only in reaction to some complaint. In short, unlike urban regions where the police are readily accessible, visible, and often proactive in patrolling and making their presence felt, in the outports the police are almost never present. Social order is maintained, perhaps more than in any other region of North America, through informal channels, by the people themselves.

In summary, the economic, political, and social contexts of the outports of Newfoundland are so qualitatively different from urban North America that it cannot be assumed that the patterns of crime and the reactions to it are the same as anywhere else.

Goal of the Study

The goal of this study is to describe and explain patterns of 'criminal' behaviour and community reactions to such behaviour in two Newfoundland outports. The main contribution is an ethnographic account, or cultural description, of acts that are deemed criminal by the rules and regulations of the state, in a part of North America that is culturally unique. It is the result of almost ten years of ongoing contact with a number of individuals, involving an extended period of field work, numerous shorter visits to Newfoundland and return visits by outport citizens to our home, and innumerable phone calls. This extensive contact has not only allowed for the development of familiarity with the local language and culture but also provided the opportunity to know, or know of, many of the local characters and events that provided the content and basis for much of what people are concerned with and talk about in the research sites.

The better to understand the cultural patterns of outport crime and deviance, the participant observation data are complemented by a description of the history of settlement and the important economic and criminal justice developments, where these are relevant. Indeed, in the late 1980s and early 1990s the outports of Newfoundland have gone through a period of rapid social change and adjustment. Finally, to give the reader a more in-depth understanding of outport crime patterns, a detailed description of the two communities that were the primary research sites is undertaken.

Review of the Rural Crime Literature

Only a small proportion of the immense criminological literature has focused on rural crime or rural policing (e.g., Warner, 1978; Smith and Huff, 1982), a situation which is no doubt due in part to the fact that rural areas have dramatically lower crime rates when measured by both police statistics and victim surveys (Laub, 1983; Lyerly and Skipper, 1981; Kaill and Smith, 1984). Much of what has been done in rural criminology is relatively recent and has focused on rural farm areas or the American South (see Warner, 1978), leaving rural non-farm areas like Atlantic Canada almost untouched by systematic criminological research.

There are some indications that the nature of the crime problem is different in rural regions. Vandalism, for example, seems to be more frequent, but there is much less gang or group crime (Smith and Huff, 1982; Phillips and Wurschmidt, 1982). Figures for Canada indicate that the rate of violation of provincial statutes is about seven times higher in rural areas than urban ones (Kaill and Smith, 1984). These are often technical violations (after Ericson, 1982) which, in subsistence fishing communities, involve fishing, hunting, and game regulations. While the topic of fishing illegality and fishery policy enforcement in Atlantic Canada has begun to be addressed (McMullan, Perrier and Okihiro, 1988; Phyne, 1990; Arai, 1994), there has been precious little study by criminologists of outport crime of any sort.

In their seminal contribution to criminological theory, Taylor, Walton, and Young (1973) described what they saw as the formal requirements for an adequate social theory of deviance. Such a theory would need to describe the situation, perceptions, and mind set of the perpetrators of the fact (the 'immediate origins' of the deviant act) and a description of the act itself. It would also need to assess the 'immediate origins of the social reaction' to the act, or the ways in which those witnessing or affected by the act classify, label, and react to it, including not only the victims and the community but also the agents of the criminal justice system and others whose actions have a bearing on the situation. Furthermore, Taylor, Walton, and Young called for social theories that place the criminal act and the reactions to it in the historical, economic, and political context in which the act, and the reactions to it, take place (the 'wider origins' of the social act and the social reactions). Only when all of these elements are tied together can a social theory of deviance be considered adequate.

For a criminologist, providing anything even remotely resembling an adequate social theory using Taylor, Walton, and Young's criteria is a rather tall and daunting order. Yet, because the culture and context of Newfoundland's outports are so different from those of urban North America, it is necessary to go beyond just a description of the behaviour of the individuals involved to arrive at an understanding of outport criminal behaviour. This study is written in the belief that an ethnographic approach must be complemented by an explicit treatment of the wider origins and context of outport life. Taylor, Walton, and Young's work thus served as an inspiration for the present work by pointing out the general requirements for an 'adequate' social theory of deviance.

Taylor, Walton, and Young's work, and the work of labelling and critical theorists in general, also served as an inspiration to this study by pointing out that the designation of what is criminal is itself problematic. In outport Newfoundland, several of the behaviours described in this study are criminal under the laws of the province or of Canada, but are not viewed as criminal by members of the outport community. Indeed, activities such as game hunting, with or without a licence, and the distilling of liquor are seen as having their moral basis in economic necessity, and/or as legitimate behaviours associated with the traditional outport way of life. This conflict between legal codes and local custom or usufruct rules is crucial to understanding patterns of outport crime and its rationalizations, motivations, and adaptations. Much of the cultural description of behaviours included in this study revolves around this conflict.

I do not claim to present an adequate theory of any particular form of outport crime in this study. Rather, this study attempts to increase our understanding of patterns of behaviour by describing both the immediate origins of the criminal acts and the reactions involved, and by providing some information on the wider origins as well.

'Classic' Studies of Outport Culture

While criminologists have almost totally ignored the outports, a fairly extensive literature, mainly anthropological, that developed during the 1960s and early 1970s described the outport culture and still provides some insight into patterns of outport crime. This literature came to prominence as part of a wider concern at that time for understanding outport culture with a view to facilitating and assessing the effects of the Newfoundland government's resettlement program, in which whole communities were moved to larger centres in an attempt to industrialize the economy (e.g., Faris, 1973; Philbrook, 1966; Firestone, 1967; Szwed, 1966; Matthews, 1975). This 'classic' outport literature has provided general descriptions of outport culture in that era.[6]

The development of a unique outport culture typically was attributed to the geographical isolation of each village, a physical isolation amplified by the development of an economic system that, historically, severely limited contact with outside persons except through the dominant local merchants. The resulting social isolation made villagers economically dependent on merchants (in a cashless mercantile or credit system) for continued participation in the fishery. The lack of adequate payment for the salt fish led to the construction of a way of life based upon individual resourcefulness and resilience, the pluralistic or foraging orientation described above, and mutual dependence on other villagers for the provision of community services. The tightly knit interpersonal web thus created was strengthened by the fact that everyone who was a member of the community (locally phrased as 'belonging to' the village) was tied into extensive and overlapping kinship and friendship relationships with almost everyone else, so one's social behaviour or misbehaviour had potentially serious implications on the whole community. As argued by

Faris (1973, 101–2), the end result was a series of rules and prescriptions which placed a premium on predictable behaviour and expected response, a prohibition on overt expressions of emotion, aggression, and exploitation, and a consequent egalitarian stress. Firestone (1967), Szwed (1966), and Sider (1980, 1986) have written the most complete descriptions of the ritualistic patterns of interaction between individuals in the outports, resulting from the need to maintain harmony and peace. The overt expression of aggression was limited to certain times or occasions, for those who were part of the moral community.

For this study, the major contribution of these classic Newfoundland outport studies has been a description of norms, rituals, and values by which social order was maintained in the outports despite an almost complete absence of regular law enforcement. These informal social control mechanisms were seen to be extremely effective at preventing overt interpersonal conflict, largely because the ultimate sanction was social death: ostracism from the community and exile into a perceived hostile world (e.g., Faris, 1973, 106).

The Current Economic Basis of Outport Life

Over the past twenty-five years, there have been many changes in the outport way of life. The grinding poverty and endless tasks associated with the salt-cod fishery have been moderated, not so much by any significant improvement in the state of the fishery from the point of view of most outport fishers (see chapter 2 for a review of fishery-related changes) as by the provision of electricity, better transportation, modern communications and conveniences like telephone and television, and government social programs. Of special importance are unemployment insurance benefits, which are paid to fishermen idled in the off-season and to the seasonally employed (fish plant workers, loggers, and low-paid non-professional service workers such as store clerks, gas station attendants, and so on) who receive at least ten weeks of paid employment. The importance of unemployment insurance is indicated below:

Unemployment insurance has become so fundamental to the well-being of outport households that the term 'unemployment' itself means unemployment insurance. It is a positive value, and households and communities co-ordinate their efforts so as to maximize the amount of unemployment insurance they receive. To qualify one member, or even better, two or more members of the household for unemployment insurance for most of the year is the fundamental priority of the outport economy, and the basic requirement for achieving sound economic security. (House et al., 1989, 46–7)

Unemployment insurance is treated as another resource, albeit the most important one, whose benefits are to be maximized personally and collectively. Receiving unemployment benefits is not stigmatized, though receiving welfare benefits is, resulting in the numbers of welfare recipients being quite low (cf. figures for two fishing communities on the Great Northern Peninsula studied by House et al., 1989, 52).

Outport life on the northeast coast of Newfoundland still revolves around seasonal activities associated with domestic production. Felt et al. (1995b) document the extensive amount of home construction, self-provisioning, and provision of unpaid work for other households they found among residents of the Great Northern peninsula of Newfoundland during 1988, and Omohundro (1993) describes in detail the daily and seasonal activities of residents of Main Brook, a northeast coast village whose economy is based more on woods work than fishing, as they go about obtaining 'rough food.'[7] Clearly, in the outports, such activity remains economically vital for the large numbers whose total cash income is low. House, White, and Ripley found that about four in five families felt that household production was very important in making a contribution.[8]

The combination of seasonal paid employment, domestic production, and unemployment insurance benefits (and other governmental social programs such as old age pensions) has helped to bring some material aspects of outport life in line with life in modern urban areas. In spite of being made from 'sticks' (locally cut trees, transported to and sawn at local sawmills for a portion of the lumber), houses are increasingly less likely to be tar-paper or particle-board clad boxes and more likely to resemble suburban houses, though generally built at a fraction of the urban cost if the labour component is omitted.[9] Modern electrical appliances and conveniences such as washers and dryers, stoves, refrigerators, freezers, microwave ovens, colour televisions, stereos, and video recorders are found in most houses, and commercial cable television programming is commonly available (cf. Felt et al., 1995a, for a statistical treatment of the standard of living on Newfoundland's Great Northern Peninsula). In the outports, families often own more than one snowmobile, pick-up trucks and sometimes cars are common, and all-terrain vehicles are becoming more popular.

It would be wrong to paint an even and generally rosy picture of material consumption in the outports. Fishermen who own larger boats (long liners) and possess the fishing licences enabling them to pursue a variety of species can accumulate considerable wealth, though the income is variable and often unpredictable. Successful fishermen are the consumption leaders in the community.[10] Their modern houses, furnishings, new vehicles, and even well-appointed cabins in the woods set the local standard.

For the others, who are the majority, hampered by low incomes obtained from small-boat fishing or fish plant work and consequent low unemployment insurance payments ('low stamps'),[11] obtaining the trappings of an urban middle-class life style means purchasing moderately priced items, often through financial sacrifice and in part motivated by the competitiveness described later in this book. With the exception of motor vehicles, people resist buying or receiving used goods such as clothing or furniture, which would quickly be noted and stigmatized in the community. For most people, the ability to afford manufactured (store-bought) material goods rests on the fact that the basic necessities of life – shelter, fuel, and food – can largely be obtained by the able-bodied through domestic production. This frees up a relatively larger proportion of what is received as cash income for the discretionary purchase of consumer goods.

There is a wide variation in the cost and quality of many of the lower-cost minor consumer items that are bought – clothing, televisions, stereos, household furnishings, even snowmobiles – making possible in a generic sense an equality of consumption among people in the outports, and between outport residents and other Canadians. Most outport residents own televisions and stereos and dress in 'store-bought' clothes, but, in many cases, these are low-cost and low-quality minor items. The purchase of larger and more costly items such as trucks or cars, or materials for house construction that cannot be produced locally, poses a problem for those with limited cash incomes. In many cases, major purchases occur when windfall profits are made, such as when employment on a construction project is secured or there is a good period of fish plant work. Partly finished houses are a common sight. It is not unusual for outport residents to arrange the purchase of a loan for a truck or a car through a finance company (at inflated prices compared to costs off the Island), only to default on it and lose the vehicle. This tendency for people to spend whatever disposable income they have, rather than save it, has its foundation in the traditional ability of outport families to be economically self-sufficient, either individually or collectively through mutual help from kin and friends,[12] and the consequent freedom of fear about the provision of the basic necessities of life.[13]

For most outport residents, consumer spending generally follows utilitarian principles. Practical items are bought which make the outport way of life a little easier. Pick-up trucks are bought because they can be used to transport logs, firewood, and snowmobiles. Certain types of snowmobiles (with long tracks) are preferred because they provide better traction for towing slides (sleds) or hauling logs out of the woods. Sturdy fibreglass open speedboats which require little maintenance are replacing hand-built wooden fishing boats. They can be used for commercial fishing and for semi-recreational pursuits that also contribute to the family larder, such as jigging cod or squid, or hunting seals. Roofing, sliding, windows, and insulation material for houses are frequent major purchases that serve important practical functions rather than display conspicuous consumption. In short, the cash income from jobs and government transfer payments is generally used to purchase major items in order to support the seasonal fishing, hunting, and gathering activities that are both the economic base and the leisure pursuits of those who, by tradition and economic necessity, are eminently practical.

In general, then, in the recent post-Confederation period, the standard of living in Newfoundland's outports has begun to approach the rest of urban North America. This has occurred largely because of a combination of unemployment insurance, participation in paid employment in seasonal, fishery, and forestry-related jobs, and continued involvement in domestic production. Unemployment insurance has been incorporated into the outport way of life, which in the economic realm emphasizes values of self-sufficiency, a jack-of-all-trades and foraging orientation, and independence. Indeed, people who rely on 'UI' and avoid the economic foraging activities of the outport way of life, who spend most of their time 'sporting around,' are stigmatized as 'lazy.'

Cultural Continuity in the Outports

Despite the significant economic and material change that has occurred in the outports, relatively few studies of recent cultural change have been done since the classic outport studies of the 1960s and 1970s – particularly of the cultural change that might have some impact on patterns of crime and social control.

In one major exception, Felt argued that, despite increasing urbanization and significant economic changes, traditional social controls continue to operate, though perhaps modified somewhat to fit new circumstances. He called this process 'cultural extension' (1987, 26). Many in

the outports embraced a 'fisherman's lifestyle,' adhering to the traditional moral order in spite of only having a peripheral connection to
fishing per se (29). Felt found that, despite criminogenic conditions such
as high unemployment, a high rate of alcohol consumption, poverty, and
the availability of firearms, rates of spousal violence were much lower in
the outports than in St John's or the United States. Among young men
with few job prospects and little attachment to the traditional culture,
overt displays of frustration and violence were rare, since 'they were
raised in the traditional order and feel bound to abide by it as long as
they are dependent upon their parents for lodging and community graces
for "make work" efforts' (43). In the absence of 'some calamitous
change in the society which destroys its intricate social structure' (46),
Felt predicted little increase in interpersonal violence.

The idea that there has been relatively little significant cultural change
in the outports with regard to key values and norms governing interpersonal relations is supported by a number of recent studies on the role of
women in fishing communities. This work has served as a corrective to
earlier androcentric social science work, particularly that which focused
on male-oriented activities and assumed male dominance and female
passivity (Neis, 1993; Murphy, 1995). While Antler (1977) documented the
emergence of alienation among women whose central role in the family
fishery had been replaced by fish plant work for wages, D.L. Davis (1979,
1988), Porter (1983), Neis (1993), and Murphy (1995) all suggest the
continuity of traditional values and orientations among women. For
example, in her study of a southwest coast community in the late 1970s,
Davis (1988) writes:

the strength of the local culture does not necessarily diminish as the locality
becomes increasingly precarious. As local people come to recognize their own
culture as distinct from others, they may come to value such distinctions as a
condition of survival. The grass widow role and the fishery ethos, romanticize the
past. They are idioms used by locals to express their difference from others and
to justify their existence in a remote, expensively serviced community. The stoic
supportive role of ideal women and the successful presentation of self as living up
to that traditional ideal pervades everyday village life and links generations to a
collective village, coast and island identity. (226)

Pointing out that the male dominance described by Faris (1973), Firestone (1967), and other earlier ethnographers was a biased result of their
preoccupation with male-oriented concerns, a number of feminists writers

stress that outport women continue to have their own spheres of influence in the kitchen (more of a public than a private place in the outports), in child rearing, and indirectly in the sphere of politics through effective information-sharing and co-operation (e.g., Davis, 1979; Porter, 1982; Murphy, 1995). Murphy (1995, 165) argues that most men and women accept the traditional ideal image of good women as 'clean, hardworking, maternal, and the caretakers of the family, the home and even the community,' reiterating Davis' (1988) observations about 'grass widows' and clean women made more than a decade earlier. Indeed, a relative social equality, 'a tradition of respect and gentleness between men and women' (Porter, cited in Neis, 1993, 194), continues to exist, based on women's indispensable contributions in both domestic labour and wage work.

Further evidence of cultural continuity comes from Porter's (1982) and Davis' (1979) analyses of women's extensive involvement in collective, co-operative activities like darts and church groups. Both authors suggest that the potential political impact of such groupings has been limited by the women's adherence to traditional views of the central importance to their lives of family matters, and by strongly enforced ideals of egalitarianism in the outports that limit any one person from seeking important decision-making powers.

Another indication of cultural continuity in the outports can be gleaned from observations of the sexual division of labour noted in the earlier classic studies. While the advent of labour-saving devices for household work and the substantial decline in family size since the 1970s have certainly reduced the amount of time and energy required of women for household and reproductive tasks, the extreme division of labour associated with traditional outport life remains. For example, Felt et al. (1995b), employing 1988 data from a representative sample of households on the Great Northern Peninsula, documented how most females, even if they are employed, continue to do most of the housework and child care without significant help from their spouses. Men still generally do the outdoor work in the pluralistic economy.

The increasing participation of women in paid labour and the spread of ideas calling for an end to discrimination based on sex have as yet only begun to affect the culture of the outports. For example, Palmer (1995a) indicates that on the northwest coast of Newfoundland, the pattern of patrilocality (having married sons move next to their fathers) remains strong despite the fact that the cod-trap fishery, which provided the economic basis for this pattern, has significantly declined in the face of new fishing technologies. In a similar vein, Neis (1993) points out that government policies such as those providing reduced or restricted unemployment benefits for women, and gendered hiring policies in fish plants, have continued the economic subjugation of women in the outports. The current state of the fishery threatens to make the economic situation of poorer women even worse, inasmuch as there are calls for the elimination of part-time and marginal workers from any future fishing industry in Newfoundland.

Finally, a number of studies have documented the strong attachment of outport residents to the traditional attractions of outport life. In spite of macro-indicators such as high unemployment rates, a high incidence of poverty, and limited community services and leisure and recreational facilities that would suggest the opposite, surveys (Richling, 1985, for Bay of Islands on Newfoundland's west coast; House et al., 1989, for two communities on the Great Northern Peninsula, and Sinclair and Felt, 1993, for the Great Northern Peninsula overall) indicate high levels of satisfaction with outport life among inhabitants. Reasons cited generally include proximity to relatives and friends, preference for a quiet and safe place to live and raise families, and nearness to outdoor activities and the physical freedom the outdoors offers. As well, outport residents' perception that 'you'd never starve here,'[14] since they can provide the necessities of life out of non-employment domestic production activities and an informal exchange of services with kin and friends, is not to be underestimated as a factor affecting preference for the outport life style. For these reasons, relatively few who have the choice leave the outports. Among those who do, most expect to return after a sojourn in mainland cities. Indeed, the rate of return migration is high, with over half of those who leave returning (Richling, 1985). The fact that they have returned after tasting life elsewhere provides unambiguous proof of an enduring preference for outport life among both those who returned and those who stayed (Gmelch and Richling, 1988).[15]

In summary, recent empirical studies suggest that the cultural foundation of outport life has changed relatively little in spite of significant outward modernization and a reduced dependence on the fishery itself. In particular, interaction patterns stressing egalitarianism and non-aggression, a rigid sexual division of labour, effective informal modes of social control, and values supporting a pluralistic foraging adaptation, hard work, and mutual help among outport residents that were described about twenty-five years ago during the classic period of outport research were still, by and large, applicable during the period of this study. This moral and cultural framework, as we shall see, strongly structures the patterns and modes of crime and deviance in the outports.

Organization of the Book

In order to provide essential background information for the reader not knowlegeable about the unique history and economy of Newfoundland, chapter 2 provides an overview, with special emphasis placed on the development of the Newfoundland fishery and associated changes in the administration of justice and policing in the province. Chapter 3 describes in detail the specific settings for this research, the outports of Main Harbour and Fish Arm.

Chapter 4 presents crime statistics to provide a means of comparing police-recorded information on the outports of Newfoundland with that of other Atlantic Canadian provinces, Canada, and the United States. These statistics, however, are critically assessed in light of the unique outport policing patterns, which have engendered peculiar culturally engrained attitudes towards the police, and the intimate social atmosphere, which effectively penalizes aggression towards others, including the reporting of crime to the police.

The specific types of crimes examined in this study are themselves partly the result of the unique geographical, historical, and economic context of the outports, and the sort of information that was accessible to the researcher. The practice of illegal hunting of game animals, especially moose and caribou, is the first crime examined in detail, in chapters 5 and 6. The prevalence of this activity among outport residents, and the conflict between community cultural norms, which generally support subsistence hunting, and the increasingly punitive attitudes of law enforcers have made poaching an important regional law enforcement issue.

Chapter 7 deals with the illegal manufacture and consumption of distilled alcoholic beverages or 'moonshine.' These practices have their roots in the geographical isolation of the outports, which made 'store-bought' liquor only sporadically available, and in a mercantile system which ensured that there was little money available for cash purchases such as liquor. Unlike poaching, however, moonshining receives little public community support, since it does not appear to fulfil legitimate individual, family, or community needs. The bulk of chapter 7 describes the ensuing patterns of manufacture and consumption of moonshine.

Interpersonal crimes are considered in some detail in chapter 8 because, in a region where there are no full-time police officers stationed and police visits are relatively rare, peace has traditionally been maintained among individuals by means of cultural norms that heavily proscribe aggression. In this chapter, incidents of interpersonal violence and the reactions of various people towards these incidents are described. Though relatively rare, they are important because they signify either a cultural channelling of frustrations and/or hostilities, or the breakdown of the informal social order of the outport.

No book on outport crime would be complete without a consideration of patterns of economic and social exploitation. Chapter 9 recounts people's perceptions of the mechanisms of economic abuse and exploitation of outport residents by merchants and fish plant owners. It also describes the manner in which some outside professionals who provide services for the community have taken advantage of their positions for their own social and/or economic advantage. The perceptions and attitudes of residents which have contributed to the perpetuation of unequal economic and social status are considered.

The final chapter provides an examination of the unprecedented outlawing of many of the traditional pluralistic economic activities that has occurred in the wake of the collapse of the ground fish stocks off the Newfoundland coast in the early 1990s. It describes the increasing regulation of economic activity affecting outport residents, the mode of enforcement of the regulations, current government adjustment policies, which have been instituted to help fishing communities deal with the moratorium on commercial fishing of crucial species instituted in 1992, and citizens' reactions to this new regime of rules and policies. Of particular interest are patterns of crime and civil disorder that either have already shown signs of emerging or threaten to erupt in the future as a result of the potentially catastrophic effect of recent events on the outport way of life.

There has been very little explicit treatment of the specific forms of crime described in this study by social scientists. The only significant sources of written information that have helped shed light on outport crime are the student papers, primarily written by undergraduate outport residents, which have been collected by Memorial University of Newfoundland and are housed in their Centre for Newfoundland Studies. These papers, and other sources of information, are mentioned in the chapters where they are relevant.

Scope of the Study

While there are elements and aspects of this study that will be relevant

Map 2
Regions of Newfoundland

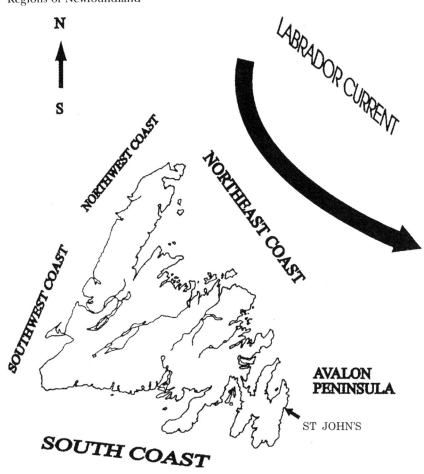

for villages throughout Newfoundland and even other parts of Atlantic Canada, a combination of geographical, climatic, economic, and historical factors suggests that the area where the study's descriptions of crime will be most valid is the northeast coast of Newfoundland. This area stretches from the tip of the Great Northern Peninsula to the Avalon Peninsula, and its fairly recent settlements are dispersed along a rugged and deeply indented coastline. Fishing, the economic backbone of the local economy, is seasonal, typically restricted from December through May or June

Map 3
The Northeast Coast of Newfoundland

by the severe winters and the cold Labrador Current, which freezes the harbours in winter and engenders ice floes in the spring and icebergs in the summer. The sea is often turbulent and always dangerous. The land is rocky and the soils poor, but there is a significant cover of mainly coniferous forests and vegetation that supports game animals such as moose and caribou. It is along the northeast coast that the seasonal round of fishing and subsistence activities described above is most relevant.[16] The Avalon Peninsula also contains fishing outports, but their proximity to St John's, the major urban centre of Newfoundland, with its urban life style, limits the extent to which the patterns of outport crime described above apply.[17]

The south coast of Newfoundland has isolated settlements like the northeast coast, but supports a year-round fishery off the Grand Banks so that the seasonal round of activity is not as pronounced. In addition, the topography is more rock-like, with generally fewer trees. Many of the villages in this area are not connected by road.

The west coast of Newfoundland has a number of farming communities in the south, to which the cultural descriptions of fishing villages do not readily apply. Along the northwest coast, though there are many similarities with the northeast coast, a year-round fishery, involving a small but very successful fleet of inshore draggers, has emerged (e.g., Phyne, 1990; Palmer, 1995a), thus somewhat limiting the extent to which the patterns described in this study might be generalized.

2

A History of Outport Settlement, Economic Development, and Law Enforcement

In order to understand outport behaviour in general, we must become at least somewhat familiar with the outports' general history. Not surprisingly, that history revolves around the salt water fishery. To understand outport patterns of crime in particular, we must delve into patterns of policing that have developed. It turns out that both the settlement and development of the outports and their history of policing are full of unique and colourful events, which are not only interesting in their own right but have contributed to the development of unique outport cultural attitudes towards law enforcement officials. The goal of this chapter is to provide a history of settlement in the outports, giving particular attention to the modes of administering justice and enforcing law that have arisen over the centuries. In addition, the chapter examines in detail the current economic developments in the Atlantic fishery and their impact on the economic and social context of life in the outports. Needless to say, except on the current economic situation, the published materials in this area are few and far between, and frequently written by non-academics.

Early Settlement in Newfoundland

The history of settlement in Newfoundland is inexorably tied in with the history of the development of the cod fishery. Indeed, in his initial sighting of Newfoundland in 1497, John Cabot noted the immense quantities of fish to be seen, and in 1498 several ships from Bristol and London set out, outfitted with fishing gear and fishermen (Prowse, 1895, 12). Shortly afterwards, however, the voyages of Gaspar Cortereal initiated Portuguese contact with the Island, and by the mid 1500s the Spanish and French had joined in the exploitation of the richest fishing grounds in the world. The ships and most of the fishermen would return home every year.

While in this very early period of Newfoundland's history most of the nations participating in the cod fishery were allies, by the late 1500s routine plundering and seizing of ships and crews by merchant adventurers, pirates, and privateers of many nationalities on the unregulated high seas resulted in cross-national tensions, but particularly between the Spanish and the British. The hostilities culminated in the attack on Britain by the great Spanish Armada in 1588. Britain's success in defeating the Armada gained them control of the transatlantic cod fishery, and, because of their seminal contribution to the naval victory of England, west country adventurers and merchants felt that they had the right to keep Newfoundland solely as a fishing possession and nothing more. They thus banded together to resist settlement, the better to retain control of the fishing grounds. With only scattered permanent European settlers, there was no need for government organization or for formal arrangements for policing.

In 1610, King James I of England granted to John Guy a charter to colonize the eastern shore of Newfoundland. Guy's colony at Cupids, Conception Bay (near the present site of St John's), was an attempt to form a farm-based community (the colonists were called planters) much like those which were to follow shortly in New England, and included a fort and a mansion. Guy was nominally the governor. The remainder of the century, however, was marked by struggles between the colonists, who initially enjoyed the support of the Crown, and the fishing interests of the English west coast adventurers and merchants who dominated the Newfoundland cod fishery. This conflict stemmed largely from the light-salted sun-dried technique of preserving fish used by the English west countrymen, which was unlike the heavily salted preservation method employed by fishermen of other nationalities. Sun drying required wood for flakes and stages (platforms constructed for holding fish) and shore facilities for drying ('rooms'). Since claims to these facilities were seasonal, with the best 'rooms' going to the first boat in the harbour, permanent settlement was a direct threat to the trans-atlantic fishery (Alexander, 1980, 18).

Despite these difficulties, by 1630 six colonies were established on the Avalon Peninsula, which was peopled mostly by humble, hard-working settlers from the west countries who settled in scattered coves and areas where safe anchorage was not possible and thus away from the hostility of the ship fishermen.

During the reign of Charles II (1660–85), west country merchant interests attempting to maintain monopolist interests in the Newfoundland fishery were able to have passed in Britain a number of orders aimed at destroying the colonial population that had already been settled for some years. In 1676 all Newfoundland settlers were to relinquish their property, an order which, not surprisingly, was resisted. In the period of escalated conflict between planters and ship fishermen that followed, some settlers moved to New England and others joined the French settlements, while in England persons sympathetic to the plight of the planters took up their cause in the political arena, but with little success. Prowse described the resulting anarchical situation in Newfoundland:

The Colony was left to drift along, a prey to every enemy. Each year the naval officers on the station made reports on the wanton aggression of the ship fisher-men, the disorders in the Island, and the need for a settled government, but it was all to no purpose. (1985, 204)

By 1698 entire control to the colony, including the administration of justice, was left in the hands of skippers of ships who were frequently illiterate: the fishing admirals, vice-admirals, and rear-admirals, who were the first, second, or third to arrive in the harbours. Prowse waxes elo-quent on the subject:

I will try and describe the fishing admiral, as he appeared to our ancestors, clothed, not in the dignity of office, not in the flowing judicial robes, not in the simple and sober black of the police magistrate, but in his ordinary blue fishing jacket and trousers, economically besmeared with pitch, tar and fish slime, his head adorned with an old sealskin cap, robbed from an Indian, or bartered for a glass of rum and a stick of tobacco. The sacred temple of law and order was a fish store, the judicial seat an inverted butter firkin. Justice was freely dispensed to the suitor who paid the most for it. In the absence of a higher bribe, his worship's decision was often favourably affected by the judicious presentation of a few New England apples. ... Time would fail to recount all the enormities and barbarities of these ignorant vulgar tyrants. They displaced the rightful owners of room, seizing them either for themselves or their friends; they fined, triangled or whipped at their pleasure every unfortunate wretch who earned their displeasure, and against whom some trumped-up charge could be made out. (1895, 226)

This description of the justice administered by the fishing admirals is corroborated by O'Neill's (1976, 550) characterization of their ways as oppressive and their punishments as harsh and partisan.

In this early period, then, it is clear that when settlement did take place in Newfoundland's outports, the settlers were a stubborn group who had to fight against the will and self-interests of fishing admirals and those who wanted control of the fishery to remain in England.

French-English Rivalry

In 1662 the French had initiated their own attempt at the colonization of Newfoundland, selecting Placentia on the Burin Peninsula as their first site and capital and centre of the fishing industry. This was part of a wider pattern of expansion by the French fishery in Nova Scotia, Cape Breton, Prince Edward Island, and elsewhere in the Gulf of St Lawrence and around Newfoundland. However, permanent settlement never took hold in Newfoundland, as the pattern of French ship fishermen coming in the spring and returning in autumn continued unabated.

The rise of the French fishery inevitably led to conflict with the British and consequently an increasing military and naval presence in Newfoundland. Open hostility soon occurred, and in 1696 and 1697 British settlements, including St John's, were invaded and destroyed, though they were never occupied for settlement by the French. The Treaty of Utrecht in 1713 temporarily ended the hostilities, with the English gaining possession of Newfoundland, but French fishermen were granted the right to build temporary huts and stages on the Treaty shore of Newfoundland, extending from Cape Bonavista in the north to Pointe Riche in the south (near Cape Ray at the southwest tip of the Island). This corresponded to the geographical distribution of the groups at the time.

Regarding law enforcement during this time of military preoccupation, Prowse writes:

The tyranny of the fishing admirals still prevailed, but it was very much tempered by the interference of the naval officers, who assumed their functions, and in a rough-and-ready way administered justice. The want of a ruler and a settled government was felt acutely at this period; representation after representation was made to the home government on the subject, and, at last, after many delays, in 1729, a Governor and Commander-in-Chief was appointed. (1895, 283)

Throughout the 1700s, competition with the French surfaced again and again. The Seven Years' War ended in the Treaty of Paris, which retained the French right to fish along the Treaty of Utrecht shore and gave over possession of the two islands of St Pierre and Miquelon. However, it also signalled that control of the fishery was to be in British hands, a situation that was solidified by the continued expansion of English settlements into the Treaty shore area. The population of Newfoundland, which was only six thousand in 1750, reached over twenty thousand by 1804 and doubled again within twelve years (Alexander, 1980, 19).

Within the colony itself, the administration of justice by the Governors was soon characterized by corruption and inequity. The practice was to appoint a Governor from the Admiralty, who then lived in St John's during the fishing season and appointed the Courts of Oyer and Terminer (Hear and Determine) and Justices of the Peace for the harbours. Most of these appointments had no salary attached, so the salaries and the constables,' clerks', and gaolers' fees were paid out of fines. This system led to immense fines for petty offences and worked primarily for the benefit of the merchants, who, particularly in the outports, had instituted the mercantile system, and to the disadvantage of the settlers, the poor, and the ethnic Irish. Even being found innocent could be costly (see O'Neill, 1976, 547). Sufficient indignation was heard in England about the need for reform that in 1791 the British Parliament passed an act establishing the Supreme Court of Juridicature of the Island of Newfoundland, an attempt to divorce court judgments from local interests.

In the outports, however, surrogate courts were held by naval officers up to 1820, when two instances of extreme unfairness (the Landergan and Butler affairs) resulted in such intense popular discontent that the present Supreme Court was instituted (O'Neill, 1976, 557). Thus the transfer of law enforcement powers to the Admiralty continued, rather than stopped, the tradition of unfair administration of justice for citizens of the outports which was a legacy of the fishing admirals. The punishment for crime in this era was similar to that found in England and other colonies. For capital punishment, the public gallows was employed, while for other offences there were stocks, pillars, branding irons, whipping, and other forms of corporal punishment (Fitzgerald, 1987).

The Period of Self-Government

Newfoundland prospered through the first part of the nineteenth century, especially during the war of 1812 between the United States and Britain. The mercantile elite of St John's particularly flourished during the long period of conflict and superseded the west country interests in the economic leadership of the fishery (Neary, 1980, 97).

Growing concerns for self-government in the colony were another product of increasing population and prosperity, but it took until 1833 for local government to be granted to Newfoundland. This is quite late when one considers that Nova Scotia obtained self-rule in 1758 and the Americans had almost always had it. The delay resulted from the omnipresent self-interest of the merchants, for whom colony status was more attractive than democratic self-rule, being more amenable to influence (cf. Neary, 1980).

Early in the period of self-government, a permanent police force began to emerge in St John's with the appointment of Sir John Harvey, a former Inspector-General of Constabulary in Ireland, as Governor, and Timothy Mitchell as Superintendent and Inspector of Police. This force replaced tavern-keepers who performed police duties in exchange for licences to operate their premises. When the British stepped up plans to remove their military garrison from Newfoundland in the 1860s, the government was compelled to organize a more efficient police force, since the garrison soldiers had previously been responsible in part for maintaining order. The Royal Newfoundland Constabulary was set up in 1872 with Head Constable Thomas Foley of the Royal Irish Constabulary selected as the head. There was no other police force on the Island (O'Neill, 1976, 574).

The period of self-rule coincides with the heyday of the traditional economy of Newfoundland. This economy was dominated by the inshore salt cod fishery, which was unfortunately notorious for its fluctuations in catch and in the market value of the catch. The 1880s is a bench-mark for the traditional economy: male employment in the catching and curing of fish reached an historic high in 1884 at sixty thousand workers, as the fishery reached its limit of growth using the existing technology, and decades of net emigration began as population growth outstripped the country's ability to provide jobs (Alexander, 1980, 23–5). Even before 1884 (see Ryan, 1980) and certainly since, spurred on by rapid population growth, the major concern of Newfoundland governments has been to reduce dependence on the fishery and to diversify the economy. During the latter part of the nineteenth century, bills were passed to encourage agriculture, manufacturing, mining, and shipbuilding and to construct a trans-Island railway. However, the original development strategy failed rather miserably (Alexander, 1980, 29–30).

The period from 1900 until the Depression, when foreign investment in Newfoundland dried up, was marked by attempts to attract international corporations through concessions such as crown land grants, lowered duties, tax holidays, and protective tariffs, with most efforts being in the area of pulp and paper, mining, and the fishery. Almost without exception, these schemes resulted in little permanent investment in or additions to the country's economy, and provision for equity participation, either private or public, was absent. The growing competitiveness of the Scandinavian salt cod industry, international tariffs on Newfoundland fish, and the development of national fishing fleets in Spain and Portugal and other countries that traditionally imported salt cod (Ryan, 1980) set the stage for the demise of responsible government and, eventually, the entrance of Newfoundland into Confederation.

The Traditional Outport Economy during Self-Government

Life in the outports in the period from actual self-rule until the Great Depression needs to be understood in economic, political, and social contexts. At the turn of the twentieth century, the bulk of the population lived in over twelve hundred small fishing settlements that dotted the six-thousand-mile coastline (McDonald, 1980, 148). There was a marked absence of both roads and farms, a situation that resulted in a lack of economic alternatives and thus lent itself to domination by merchants (Sider, 1980). In the fishery, truck payment, in which fish were exchanged for commodities without cash, and the 'tal qual' method, in which all the fish in the community were bought by the merchant at one average price regardless of the quality of the curing (to help speed the fish to market), were in full operation (McDonald, 1980; Sider, 1980). The advent of steamships and the railway, combined with the bank crash of 1894, which had weakened the position of St John's merchant houses as direct suppliers of fishermen, heralded the rise of a new class of outport merchants who exerted a 'less obvious, more indirect yet more powerful control of rural commerce' (McDonald, 1980, 150). Fishermen were tied to the local merchant by the credit system of supply, were often in debt, rarely received written accounts, and were at the mercy of the merchants regarding the quality and price of the fish catch. Many families supplemented their fishing efforts with small vegetable gardens. Sider describes the annual round of economic activities:

Each family grew a few vegetables for their own use in their own garden plot, knitted their own nets, and built and repaired their own houses and boats. Families cooperated occasionally with each other, but outside the fishery they did this more in the exchange of certain skills – craftsmen helping to repair a boat; women assisting each other at birth – than in the sharing of ordinary, routine labour. Outside the fishery, people sometimes pursued economically necessary activities in the company of one another. Women went berry-picking with one another, each for their own table. Men would go off in the Fall to gather firewood together, or to hunt together, each bringing home their own, except perhaps occasionally in a shared hunt. Men would also go off together, upon occasion, to work a few weeks on a spring sealing boat, or spend a few Fall months in a logging camp, but often they sought out these sources of a small cash income by themselves. (1980, 20)

The scattered pattern of settlement meant there was no tax base for local government, and also made the provision of government services very expensive. Because of the savings involved, it became the practice of successive Newfoundland governments to delegate public responsibilities to other agencies: education and health to Church and missionary organizations, transportation to private companies, and so on. McDonald writes:

The distribution of public works moneys, relief and welfare benefits was assigned by the government to assembly members, local clergymen, magistrates, government heelers, and politically-appointed relief officers. It is true that in most cases the inadequate tax bases of rural settlements had resulted in there being no local government outside St John's, but the practice of having the central government or church authorities control all appointments to local road and church school boards did much to sharpen the authoritarian and remote image the government projected to the ordinary outport residents. Not surprisingly, there existed in the outports a deep resentment of having their destinies controlled in all things, no matter how indirectly, by a distant and alien capital that financed itself though a heavy and severely regressive customs tariff, which impinged most on those least able to bear it. (1980, 154)

With their unchallenged economic power, then, the local merchants, along with the clerics who assumed important administrative tasks for the government and often acted as intermediaries between individuals and a distant government, had a domineering influence on all aspects of outport life. This situation was exacerbated by the firm establishment of government funding distributed on the basis of political and financial favour, a system that was accepted by politicians and the electorate (Elliot, 1980, 186).

The Commission of Government and the Newfoundland Rangers

The collapse of self-government in Newfoundland has been attributed both to corruption and irresponsible government spending on the one hand (Elliot, 1980), and to unfortunate economic developments on the other. The war demand from 1914 and 1918 did not do much to diversify the economy, which was still overwhelmingly dependent on the export of primary products, and in addition decimated the labour force and increased debt, since the country financed much of its war effort in New York and London (Alexander, 1980, 35). The trans-Island railway was another major financial drain on the economy, and to make matters worse, the stagnation of trade experienced after the war crippled the economy and increased the demand for emergency relief.

By 1932, it was clear that the government of Newfoundland would be unable to meet interest payments on its debt and, indeed, it was saved from default only by the assistance of Canada and the United Kingdom. The same year the Amulree Royal Commission was appointed, and in 1933 it reported, laying blame for the finances on extravagant expenditures and political abuses of the past (cf. O'Neill, 1976; Elliot, 1980). Elliot writes of the reaction of Newfoundlanders to the Amulree Commission report:

So willing were they to accept this judgment of themselves, that the possibility of default was only briefly considered. Instead, with almost shameless docility, even eagerness, the Newfoundland government accepted the recommendations of the commission on behalf of the people of the colony, and made themselves a party to the suspension of responsible and democratic government. ... The profound sense of moral inferiority and ineptitude that was established in 1924 left little doubt in the minds of the colony's people that they were indeed unfit to govern themselves, particularly since it was again being stated explicitly before all the world in 1933. (1980, 199)

Following the Amulree Commission's recommendations, the Newfoundland government requested that a Commission of Government be established, temporarily, until Newfoundland could get back onto its own feet, with political power vested in a Governor and the British government assuming responsibility for finances.

The Commission of Government concerned itself with every act of the government which involved the spending of money, including the appointment of even minor officials. Based on a recommendation that a force be established along the lines of the Royal Canadian Mounted Police, who not only policed but also administered customs acts, assisted in the post office and railway, and so on (Crane, 1982, 2), the Commission of Government established the Newfoundland Rangers in 1935. Horwood describes their mandate as follows:

The Rangers were not only to act as the first rural police force in Newfoundland, and as servers and protectors of forests, game and fisheries, but also as liaison between the people and the government. Some such liaison had become necessary with the passing of responsible government at the end of 1933. Up to that time, the members of the House of Assembly had acted as liaison between their constituents and the power centre at St. John's. In their ridings they had, in fact, more power than we should now think proper. They did such things as distribute public works money, appoint postal carriers and postmaster; they often made arrangements between St. John's merchants and outport agents. Their sudden disappearance from the political scene left many outport people without any contact with St. John's, except, perhaps, through a minister or a priest. The Rangers were to fill this role along with all the others. (1986, 13–14)

The Rangers were set up under the Department of Natural Resources with Captain L.T. Stick appointed Chief Ranger, and RCMP officer F.A. Anderson in charge of training, which included tasks associated with six different government departments. In 1935–6 sixteen detachments were opened along the northeast coast from Twillingate to Bonne Bay and in Labrador, with none along the south coast or on the Avalon Peninsula. Crane, himself a Ranger, wrote that, in short order,

the Rangers had become accepted and trusted throughout the Island and Labrador. Without elected representation, the Rangers became the sole link between the people and government and were called upon to solve many and complex problems. They had no recourse to higher authority because of the severe lack of communications, so they made decisions and lived with them. (1982, 5)

During the Second World War, their duties expanded to include issuing National Registration cards, administering the aircraft and submarine watch, and providing security for Gander Air Force base. With Confederation, the Ranger force was disbanded in 1950, and serving members were given the option of transferring to the RCMP. During this time, the Royal Newfoundland Constabulary diminished in size and were finally restricted to the City of St John's and some highway patrol work (O'Neill, 1976, 576).

Confederation

During the Second World War, many of the resources of Newfoundland were earmarked to aid the war effort, but shortly afterwards, Newfoundland's economy, which relied heavily on earnings from overseas export, was in danger. Virtually all of Newfoundland's salt cod fish exports went to soft currency countries in western Europe and elsewhere. With devalued and devaluing currencies against the dollar, many of these countries bought fewer Newfoundland fish or stopped importing it at all (Alexander, 1980).

Meanwhile, led by Richard Cashin's fiery calls for independence, there was a growing movement to have Newfoundland return to Dominion status. This led to an election of delegates, including Joseph Smallwood representing Gander, to a National Convention to choose the form of government best suited to the needs of Newfoundland. The convention proposed a referendum that included the option of confederation with Canada. The confederationists won by a small margin, and on 31 March 1949 Newfoundland became the tenth Canadian province.

The 1949 provincial election gave the pro-Confederation Liberals an overwhelming majority, with Smallwood becoming Premier, a situation which did not change for the next twenty years. Smallwood's position of influence in the first two decades of Newfoundland's experience in Confederation was ensured by the extension to the Island of Canadian social welfare programs, which instantly and substantially improved the standard of living. In addition to the family allowances and old age pensions, a greatly expanded health care system and improved educational opportunities won Smallwood not only political support but also a very strong personal following. Depicting himself as a 'man of the people' and employing skilful public-speaking techniques, Smallwood made frequent use of radio and television appearances to gain unparalled powers in the province.

Developments in the Fishery since Confederation

As noted in chapter 1, the post-Confederation period in Newfoundland has been marked by significant change in the Atlantic fishery. In this section, major changes, many of which have been the result of international developments, are described. These developments are important to understand because they have affected the economic base and social structure of the outports and because they have resulted in increasing state intervention in the mode of fishing and the pursuit of subsistence activities in the outports.

In the 1950s, the Atlantic fishery was changed forever by the emergence of a new, much more efficient technology for dealing with fish. Factory freezer trawlers, which operated year round, began plying the largely unregulated waters around Newfoundland. These new ships were part of the distant water fleets of countries like Britain, Spain, Portugal, Japan, the USSR, and Poland. As Neis (1991, 157) points out, they employed a mass production strategy, depending for their efficiency on a large, dependable supply of relatively homogeneous raw materials, fish stocks which were found in only a few places in the world. Their product, semi-processed fresh and frozen fillets and fish blocks, were consumed by a growing market of people interested in foods which could be quickly prepared using rapidly spreading kitchen items such as electric appliances.

With the loss of markets for salt fish after the Second World War noted above, the major product of Newfoundland's outports increasingly became fresh and frozen fish fillets. While the traditional methods of fishing using fixed gear (cod traps and hand lines) did not change much in the inshore fishery of Newfoundland, the mode of processing did. To process the local catch, fish plants sprang up in many outports, supplanting family-based dried salt cod preparation with a wage-based factory style of fish preparation. Sider (1986) dates the end of the traditional salt cod fishery at 1960.

The building of fish plants in outports was necessitated by the need to process locally caught fresh fish quickly. Some larger plants operated year round, supplied by offshore trawlers and by inshore fishers which could, combined, provide a more steady supply of fish. In other communities, the uncertain and seasonal supply of fish required more flexible supplies of labour. The resettlement of whole fishing communities during this period helped fill this need (Neis, 1991).

Lured by Smallwood's slogan, 'Burn your boats boys, there will soon be two jobs for every man' (Sider, 1980, 180), the long-impoverished residents of many outports signed petitions during the 1960s for relocation to 'growth centres' where they would presumably be in a position to take part in the industrialization and modernization of Newfoundland's economy and have access to better schools and services (e.g., Economic Council of Canada, 1980, 19; Overton, 1980, 48). Needless to say, this relocation of whole communities failed spectacularly in its promise of providing non-fishery-related jobs (e.g., Royal Commission on Employment and Unemployment, 1986, 49). However, it did increase the supply of local fish-plant workers, especially women and younger men, who could be hired seasonally and temporarily.

This emergence of fish plants in the outports did little to change most citizens' situation of economic dependence. Dependence on the merchant in the cashless salt cod fishery was simply replaced by dependence on low-paid fish plant work for employment. Neis (1991) documents how this came about:

Plants were often built in relatively isolated communities, giving firms a monopoly in the local markets for both labour and fish (fresh fish is highly perishable). The decentralized structure of firms with plants located in several communities and regions enhanced this control. By owning several plants and relying on corporate trawlers and owner-operated enterprises, management increased its control over individual groups of workers and fishers. Multiplant ownership limited the ability of workers in single communities to strike for higher wages because vessels could be diverted to alternative plants, and companies could increase their reliance on fish derived from or processed in a different sector.

Other mechanisms of control included nepotistic, sectarian and gendered hiring practices; varying degrees of corporate ownership of other businesses in the community; or effective control of housing, electrical power, water supplies or municipal governments. These varying mechanisms often contributed to the development of close ties between community and work that interfered with the development of industrial unionism. Such development was, at any rate, discouraged by existing labour legislation under which fishers and trawler workers did not have the right to unionize. (162–3)

During the 1960s the total catch of fish around Newfoundland increased dramatically, reaching a peak of 807,000 metric tons of northern cod, the primary species, in 1968 (Schrank et al., 1992, 342). For outport fishermen, however, the prices paid for their catch remained low, partly because of competition with low-cost trawler-caught fish, and partly because of control over prices by fish plant owners. In addition, inshore catches were increasingly limited by competition for fish from the offshore sector. A Department of Fisheries and Oceans report at this time estimated the average income of inshore fishermen on Newfoundland's east coast and in Labrador at $1500 from fishing (Schrank, 1995 289). As mentioned in chapter 1, the development of Fishermen's Unemployment Insurance, based on the assumption that they were employees of merchants and fish plant owners, significantly evened out and supplemented fishermen's and fish plant workers' incomes. Fishermen's UI also enabled fish plant operations based on seasonal and low-paid wage work to retain a cheap, local labour supply.

In the late 1960s, over-harvesting of ground fish by foreign trawlers led to catches that by 1971 were only about half of what they had been in

1968. Combined with a drop in demand for fish caused by the oil-related recession of the early 1970s, the ensuing crisis resulted in efforts through the International Commission for the Northwest Atlantic Fishery (ICNAF) to introduce national quotas, and in the convening of the Third United Nations Conference on the Law of the Sea in 1973. Following this convention, Canada declared Extended Fisheries Jurisdiction (EFJ) over a two-hundred-mile zone off the Atlantic coast beginning 1 January 1977, with the intention of displacing the foreign trawler fleets.

The declaration of the EFJ and increasing catches and fish prices just prior to 1977 resulted in an unprecedented air of optimism surrounding the Canadian inshore fishery. Motivated by a general belief that the fishery should be conducted by full-time professional fishermen who could earn a respectable income from their efforts (e.g., Matthews and Phyne, 1988; A. Davis, 1991), federal and provincial governments instituted loan and grant policies enabling fishermen to modernize their boats. Within two years, the Newfoundland Fisheries Loan Board payments for inshore vessel subsidies went from $3.55 million to $11.91 million (Schrank et al., 1987, 549). From 1976 to 1980, the number of registered inshore vessels more than doubled, to 19,594 (Schrank, 1995, 291). This program resulted in the construction of a sector of larger (thirty-five to sixty-five feet in length), more mobile vessels or 'long liners,' which were felt to be commercially viable, but whose costs (around $50,000) were approximately ten times the cost of the smaller boats used to that time.

Motivated by perceptions of bright prospects for employment in a Canadian-controlled fishery, high unemployment levels, and a desire among most Newfoundlanders to stay in their own communities (see chapter 1), many opted for employment in the fishery, and the numbers ballooned from 13,736 in 1975 to 33,640 in 1980 (Schrank, 1995, 291). The fishery served as an 'employer of last resort.' The rise in fish prices and occasional labour shortages in community plants in this period (Neis, 1991) resulted in increasing unionization by the Newfoundland Fishermen, Food and Allied Workers Union, and, under a Liberal fisheries minister, Romeo Leblanc, who was sympathetic to the inshore sector (Fairley, 1990, 177), the inshore portion of the total catch increased and wages at fish plants rose.

This period of good times in the Newfoundland fishery was short-lived. The near shore fleet, consisting of long liners which could roam much further from home and employed a combination of fixed and mobile gear (especially gill nets), squeezed out the smaller boats of the inshore

sector. Because of the necessity of paying back loans and the internaliza-
tion of a more selfish, businesslike orientation to fishing (Davis, 1991), a
more rapacious, fish-hunting attitude developed in this sector. These
changes, along with continued offshore overfishing and another recession
in the United States, which affected the American market for fish,[1] caused
another collapse in the Atlantic fishery in the early 1980s.

To deal with this new crisis, the Canadian government appointed a task
force (the Kirby Commission). This led to the massive financial restructuring of the industry. Smaller fish plants in Newfoundland were consolidated into Fishery Products International (FPI), in which the government
took a strong equity position.[2]

A few years of good catches recurred in the mid-1980s. However, despite the displacement of foreign fishing boats, the inshore catches
increased only slightly. The bulk of the catch went to the Canadian
offshore sector (including FPI), whose catch multiplied from 3100 tons
in 1976 to 118,000 tons in 1986 (Schrank et al., 1992, 347). The offshore
segment benefited from government policies and grants which reflected
views that the inshore fishing fleet was inefficient and obsolete (Williams
and Theriault, 1990, 107). Within the inshore segment, by the end of the
1980s, long liner owners and their employees accounted for almost half
of the output of the inshore fishery and in some cases were making a lot
of money (Fairley, 1990, 172). In contrast to this class, about one-third of
all Newfoundland fishermen in 1990 made less than $10,000 from all
sources of income (Task Force on Incomes and Adjustment in the Atlantic Fishery, 1993, 8).[3]

While the Atlantic fishery as a whole suffered from ups and downs, the
non-fishery component of the outport economy seems to have endured
only setbacks since the end of the 1970s (Royal Commission on Employment and Unemployment, 1986, 49–50). The construction boom associated with the infusion of government money to modernize Newfoundland
and with large-scale resource-extraction projects like the dam at Churchill
Falls, Labrador, petered out, and mechanization of the logging industry
reduced employment in the woods. The European ban on seal imports
destroyed that industry. Jobs in other provinces dried up during a long
period of economic stagnation and occasional recession, resulting in the
return migration of some Newfoundlanders.

This then, was the state of the Newfoundland outport economy at the
start of the research for this study. In 1986, the official unemployment
rate of rural Newfoundland was 24.6 per cent, about twice the national
average. In the most comprehensive survey of an outport, the real unem-

ployment figure was pegged at 39 per cent (Royal Commission on Employment and Unemployment, 1986, 49). The fishery, however, was relatively buoyant with a resurgence of good landings combined with a good market for sea products (Hinds, 1995, 276–7).

From 1988 through 1992, the resource base of the Newfoundland fishery declined catastrophically, collapsing to one-quarter of the 1988 total. In July 1992, a complete moratorium on commercial fishing of the northern cod was introduced and it is expected to remain in place until the end of the 1990s. For the northeast coast of Newfoundland this has amounted to economic devastation, with the loss of employment and income for virtually all of the twelve thousand fishermen and fifteen thousand plant workers (Task Force on Income and Adjustment in the Atlantic Fishery, 1993, 22). The subsequent closure of even the recreational or subsistence fishery, increasingly severe enforcement of laws against and punishment for illegal hunting of game animals, and, in some areas, restrictions on cutting down of trees have rendered an entire population idle and nearly totally reliant on federal government funds allocated from a Fishery Adjustment program that was hastily introduced in 1992 and superseded by a similar program in May of 1994.

A description of these recent events, subsequent changes in fishery enforcement, and the resultant impact on crime and social order is provided in chapter 10.

The Post-Confederation Policing Structure

With Confederation, a new era in the structure of law enforcement began in Newfoundland. The self-policing of the outports or minimal policing by the Newfoundland Rangers has slowly given way to policing administered by government bodies, as in the rest of North America. In the area of the fisheries, for example, the Canadian government, through the agency of the Department of Fisheries and Oceans, took over responsibility for policy and enforcement in the salt water fishery (see chapter 10). A treatment of developments in the administration of game and wildlife laws, currently a responsibility of the provincial government, is given separately in chapter 5, which deals with poaching.

Confederation brought significant changes to general policing. The Newfoundland Rangers were disbanded, though many of them and some of the Newfoundland Constabulary were absorbed into the RCMP. Upon entry into Confederation, Newfoundland, like other provinces of Canada where there is no provincial police force, entered into an agreement to have the RCMP do its provincial policing (McGrath and Mitchell, 1981, 45).[4] The Royal Newfoundland Constabulary's jurisdiction was limited, shortly after the war, to St John's.

Unlike most other provinces, Newfoundland has not consolidated its policing legislation into a single Police Act, and, indeed, has retained the Newfoundland Company of Rangers Act, though it is not in effect. By 1985 a total of 943 police officers were serving the province, 60 per cent being members of the RCMP primarily under provincial contract, 39 per cent belonging to the Royal Newfoundland Constabulary, and the remainder a handful of Ports Canada and Canadian National Railway Police (Statistics Canada, 28).[5]

With the assumption of outport policing by the RCMP, that organization's considerable financial, organizational, and symbolic resources have been brought to bear on local law enforcement. RCMP officers are recruited nationally, given the most extensive professional training of any police force in Canada, and often posted for relatively short periods to isolated outport detachments. Like all other providers of government services in rural Newfoundland, however, they are limited in effectiveness by the fact that most residents live in small, dispersed, and isolated communities, travel to which is frequently hampered by poor weather and roads.[6]

Summary

Throughout the history of Britain's oldest colony, patterns of settlement have been strongly affected by the policies and behaviours of various groups as they have attempted to control and exploit the cod fishery. In the early period, the west country fishing interests actively discouraged settlement, in part by allowing the administration of justice to be determined by fishing admirals. Subsequently, law enforcement by the Admiralty was initiated, but the justice administered continued to be partisan and unfair, serving to penalize the interests of permanent settlers.

During the period of self-government, perennial financial problems in Newfoundland's fishing-based economy left the outports with few social or policing services provided by government. The institution of the credit system forced most outport citizens to supplement their incomes by a variety of seasonal hunting and gathering activities which, in the absence of any effective policing agency, were controlled informally, if at all. This neglect worked to the advantage of those who profited from the credit system. People were almost totally isolated from government influence.

Despite great changes in the salt water fishery since Confederation, most outport residents still earn low, seasonal, and unstable incomes. People must still make pluralistic economic adaptations, which maintain and reinforce values of self-sufficiency and mutual aid and participation in the activities of the outport way of life. The transfer of control of policing to a bureaucratic federal police force has had so far only a limited direct effect on citizens, owing to the dispersal of the population into small, isolated communities where law enforcement officials are only sporadically present. For the most part, informal mechanisms are still paramount in importance for understanding patterns of crime and social order in the outports. It is important to note, however, that the community-based controls on behaviour developed partly because of the historical mistreatment of outport residents, which has affected cultural attitudes towards law enforcement officials. Chapter 4 describes the deeply engrained fear and suspicion of powerful strangers in the outports, and most of the other chapters describe how the behaviour of those engaged in crime, and the reactions of the rest of the community to criminal transgressions, have been affected by attitudes and orientations which have their roots in the unique patterns of settlement and law enforcement experienced in the outports.

3

The Setting

The field work in this study was undertaken in two research sites, Main Harbour and Fish Arm.[1] Main Harbour and Fish Arm are located about forty sea miles apart on one of Newfoundland's rugged peninsulas jutting out into the Atlantic Ocean on the northeasterly side of the triangle-shaped island (see map 2). The two communities are neighbouring in the sense that there is no other major settlement separating them,[2] owing to the harshness and impassability of the coastal terrain and the abandonment of many smaller communities during the resettlement program described earlier. Main Harbour is located near the most inland point of Northern Bay, the large bay separating this peninsula from the next; Fish Arm is further out in the bay. A ferry service connects the two settlements, operating twice a week except in winter, and solidifying the social connections between them. Indeed, it is interesting to note that practically all contacts with people from outside the community follow the lines of the ferry service up and down the bay. Almost no contact occurs with the settlements across the bay, which are less distant. This situation has probably been reinforced by the fact that the organization of medical services, religious services, mail and other government services, and even policing, as well as kinship ties, have followed the same pattern up and down each coastline of the bay, rather than across.

A boat journey along the Northern Bay coast reveals a fjord-like topography of steeply rising cliffs of granite and gneiss, scoured by the elements, with few areas of level land on the shore. Some of the highest hills in Newfoundland are found here, rising to elevations in some cases well more than one thousand feet. The hills are forested primarily with coniferous trees, especially spruce and balsam fir, among which are interspersed a few of the hardier deciduous trees, notably birch. Indeed, pulpwood logging has been the primary source of employment other than fishing and fish-related industries, and there have been a number of local small-scale lumbering enterprises that have waxed and waned throughout this century. The recent improvement of a gravel 'highroad' ('highway') from the Trans-Canada Highway to Main Harbour has removed the major obstacle to large-scale exploitation of the timber resources – the lack of forest access roads – so that at the time of this writing, some fairly long-term plans to log the region around Main Harbour were underway. The smaller community of Fish Arm is not connected by road to any other community, and there are no plans as yet for this to happen in the near future.

As well as coniferous forest, the hills in this area of Northern Bay support a number of fruits and berries, which are picked in the appropriate season – red currants, blueberries, squash berries, blackberries, and raspberries are the local names for the most abundant types – while nearby barren areas provide some partridge berries. The hills are dissected by streams and rivers and numerous ponds and 'meshes' (marshes), some of which are used as sources of drinking water for the communities. The elevated topography of the inland area has resulted in a barrens-like environment that is home to a small number of caribou. The other notable wildlife includes moose, rabbit, fox, beaver, and bear, as well as a number of birds.

Sociologically, it is important not to discount the effect of steep, high, and unpopulated terrain that is practically impassable except by arduous climbs on foot or using rackets (snowshoes), or more recently by snowmobile. Except for occasional forays by the men for logging, hunting, or recreational purposes, and by men and women for berry picking, there is little interest in anything that might be happening beyond the first set of hills. After all, beyond the closest hills are simply more of the same, or an equally socially barren tundra.[3] Attention is thus channelled towards the sea, and inevitably on the activities of people in the immediate neighbourhood. Perhaps even more than in other isolated communities in Newfoundland, the mountains provide a physical and perceptual barrier to communication and concern for anything other than local social life.

The climate of the area has also had a major impact on patterns of settlement and activity on Northern Bay. Other than latitude, the major factor affecting the research site, and indeed the entire northeast coast of Newfoundland, is the Labrador Current, a large body of cold water flowing south from Labrador. Winters are long and cold, the arrival of spring conditions being delayed by extensive ice floes in May and into June. The temperature of the sea is close to freezing well into May, depressing the air temperatures on the coastal settlements with resulting July mean temperatures between ten and sixteen degrees Celsius (cf. Firestone, 1967, 4). It is not unusual to see icebergs at any time in the summer, and dipping one's hand in the waters for more than a few seconds even in the summer can be an exercise in physical endurance. Jackets are worn on all but the hottest summer nights.

Average January temperatures are minus twelve to minus nine degrees Celsius. Snow usually remains on the ground from December through late March or April, and can be spotted in shady locations in the hills much later in the season than that. While Northern Bay does not freeze over completely, the protected waters around Main Harbour and Fish Arm do, allowing some harbour and cove sections to be used for local winter transportation via snowmobile, walking, or rackets, and even for the landing of small planes equipped with skis. This is not without its dangers, as several snowmobiles and even an airplane have been lost when the wind or sea currents have changed, shifting the ice and opening sections of sea water. In Main Harbour, several respondents told of one teenager who lost his life when he fell off the back of a snowmobile which encountered an unexpected opening in the ice at night.

The subarctic winter conditions in this area have helped foster a peculiar pattern of geographical mobility for some residents. There have been a number of individuals who have moved to, and in some cases returned from, the Northwest Territories, and there is a smaller pattern of in-migration from small communities along 'the Labrador' which experience similar climatic conditions. Certainly the pull of having kin who can help a person get established is important in promoting this type of chain migration, but so too is the transferability of skills and orientations which allows for adaptation to the environment. Thus, one returnee spoke in very positive terms about being able to 'live' on his snowmobile in the Northwest Territories, and being able to hunt and cut wood 'just like home.' Similarly, a few persons originally from small coastal fishing villages in Labrador have married Fish Arm women and have been among the few outsiders other than professionals (mainly teachers, doctors, nurses, and ministers) to become part of the regular labour force in the community (cf. House et al., 1989).

Owing to their location at the foot of high hills and cliffs, Main Harbour and Fish Arm get a large number of sunny days, both summer and winter, compared to many other settlements on the northeast coast of

Newfoundland.[4] There is a general consternation at the nightly CBC (Canadian Broadcasting Corporation) televised weather forecast and weather bulletins on the radio, which are considered unreliable. These forecasts tend to produce a general picture for a wide area, and at best ignore conditions in the sparsely populated area of research. At any rate, a few days of travel through the area are enough to convince anyone that conditions at any place on any given day are strongly affected by the high hills forming the major feature of the local topography. The fishermen, for whom the weather is a critical occupational concern, carefully monitor the wind strength and direction 'outside' or on the main body of water in Northern Bay (which can be much different from that found immediately in the small, protected coves where settlement occurs). For a number of male respondents, winter was the favourite season, and March in particular the favourite month because there was more time to pursue one's own interests (summer being the fishing season, or the period when one attempted to collect enough 'stamps' or weeks of work to become eligible for unemployment insurance benefits), there was usually a good base of snow on the ground for snowmobiling or hunting, and the days were usually sunny.

Main Harbour

Main Harbour is a community of about seven hundred persons,[5] located a few kilometres from two islands hugging the shore of Northern Bay. According to one local historian, Main Harbour became an important local centre of population because the two islands partially blocked the flow of the ocean at the very bottom, or most inland part of Northern Bay, with the result that the water freezes earlier and thaws later there, a fact which in the past prevented the schooners that were so vital for outport supplies from landing any further down the bay. With a slightly longer ice-free harbour, Main Harbour thus eventually became a key trading centre for a large part of this area of Northern Bay.

Local legend has it that the area was close to the site of an Indian settlement. Subsequently, the area was part of the French Shore[6] and was used by French fishermen to dry their fish. There are no people of Indian, French, or jack-a-tar[7] origins in Main Harbour today, however. The first English-speaking settlers were fishermen from other parts of Newfoundland (Puddester, n.d., 2; Hewitt, 1978, 1, and other local sources) who arrived in the early 1890s[8] (settlement here, as elsewhere in Newfoundland, having been retarded by British policy forbidding permanent

TABLE 3.1
Population Growth of Main Harbour

Year	Population
1901	87
1911	143
1921	230
1935	319
1945	379
1961	422
1966	450
1971	491
1976	480
1983	750[a]
1995	650[b]

Sources: Government of Newfoundland and Labrador Censuses to 1945, and Statistics Canada from 1961 through 1976.
[a]estimate based on 2 local sources noted above.
[b]from sign posted by Town Council.

residence), and the descendants of the first few families remain an important part of the local population, judging on the basis of last names alone. The area has experienced a slow population change over the decades (see table 3.1.).

Historically, Main Harbour has been dependent on the inshore fishery, and apparently few residents have left to pursue the offshore Labrador fish stocks (Puddester, n.d., 3). Fishermen rowed out to the nearby fishing grounds daily during the fishing season, which runs from around May to November or December. All fishing and other supplies were brought in by schooner, mainly from St John's, and traded in return for surplus fish, primarily cod but also salmon. Surplus cash was a rare luxury. The first resident fish-buying and merchant operation was started by a wealthy family from another part of Newfoundland, who, according to several local sources, brought in their own employees and servants and soon dominated the economic and social life of the community. With the advent of this merchant and subsequently some competitors, Main Harbour life was probably similar to that in other communities that were geographically isolated and economically dependent on local merchants for all the necessities and consumer goods which could not be made or obtained in the small settlement itself. For decades, the inshore fishery waxed and waned, dependent primarily on seasonally variations in cod and salmon landings, and this pattern remained unchanged until the late

1970s when some fishermen began to employ long liners. The new fishing method, and the exploitation of stocks of other ground fish such as redfish, lumpfish and capelin, and, importantly, crab, have substantially increased the number directly involved in fishing (cf. Newfoundland and Labrador Hydro, 1980, 13).

Perhaps the most important development affecting the economic life of Main Harbour has been the development and expansion of the two fish plants, which together provide the major source of employment, hiring hourly paid employees, the majority women, during the fishing season from May to around December. These plants process fish from neighbouring communities on Northern Bay as well as that caught by local fishermen and truck the finished product – frozen fish or crab, by and large – to larger centres via the upgraded gravel road[9] connecting with the Trans-Canada Highway. These plants, combined with a recent large-scale construction project in the region, made employment prospects in Main Harbour very good in the early period of the research, enabling the community until very recently to retain a large proportion of its younger generation, individuals who in other years might have been forced by the lack of jobs to leave for larger centres on and off Newfoundland. Together with a number of persons who have moved to Main Harbour from nearby communities for employment, these two factors help account for the substantial increase in population of Main Harbour in the early 1980s (see table 3.1). The downturn in the fishery culminating in the moratorium on commercial ground fishing probably accounts for the loss of population over the past few years.

Although it started out as a fishing community, in fairly short order logging became an important economic activity in Main Harbour, with the establishment in 1904 of a sawmill owned by a firm in St John's. By the 1921 census, there was $54,000 worth of timber sawn and another $1500 worth of pulpwood, compared to the total value of fish products of about $17,000 (Newfoundland Colonial Secretary's Office, 1923, 241, table 2; 154–60, tables 4 and 5; 315, table 3). A number of small-scale sawmill operations have come and gone in Main Harbour, employing by 1976 thirty men (compared to twenty-one men in the fishery). In recent decades, a number of men from Main Harbour have been employed as loggers, working seasonally from January to March and from June to mid-November. These woodsmen leave Main Harbour and live in logging camps, usually returning for weekends only. Some loggers have in recent years found seasonal employment in Nova Scotia woods. During the period of research, logging has begun in the Main Harbour area and provided some jobs to local residents who wish to work closer to home.

In addition to fishing and logging, people in Main Harbour in the past grew vegetables not only for their own consumption but to sell to other nearby communities such as Fish Arm. In 1945 Main Harbour produced 2082 bushels of potatoes, 112 bushels of turnips, 10,560 bushels of cabbage, and significant amounts of beets, carrots, and hay (*Rounder*, 1979, 31), making it by far the most important local supplier of these Newfoundland dietary staples. Various forms of livestock were also raised, including sheep, cows, goats, and horses. By 1976, however, Main Harbour had only five acres of land under production, for domestic use only (ibid.),[10] and only one horse, which was used, if at all, for recreational purposes. During the period of research, there was no commercial growing or livestock production of any sort noted in Main Harbour.

It is clear from table 3.1 that the overall population of Main Harbour has grown rather slowly over its one-hundred-year history of anglophone settlement. Given the historical pattern of large family size, this has been the result largely of steady emigration of individuals (particularly women, given patterns of patrilocality) and families to other larger centres both on and off the island. Practically everyone in both Main Harbour and Fish Arm can point to kin now residing in neighbouring communities, and in the only cities in Newfoundland, Corner Brook and St John's, who visit or keep in touch by letter or telephone. The completion of the seventy-kilometre 'highroad' in the early 1950s, a dangerous, low-grade gravel side road originally built to expedite logging, ended the absolute isolation of Main Harbour and facilitated its development as a fish processing centre, providing one of the few impetuses to population growth. Subsequent decisions in the 1950s and 1960s by the Newfoundland government to centralize government services and especially to close schools then existing in tiny nearby fishing settlements were another spur to growth, but, by and large, the pattern of substantial numbers of youths and adults forced to leave the community, often seasonally or temporarily but sometimes permanently, remains relatively unabated today.

Physical Layout

The community of Main Harbour, situated on a sheltered arm or cove indenting Northern Bay, stretches approximately four kilometres from the 'bottom,' or head of the cove, to a point where the gravel main road, which generally follows the shoreline, ends abruptly at an impassable cliff.

Just beyond this point is a lighthouse overlooking the point at which the cove meets the larger body of water of Northern Bay. This main road is an extension of the gravel 'highroad' one must negotiate to reach the town.

Most of the houses and non-residential buildings have been built on either side of the main road. Owing to the irregular location of the steep hills, they have varying amounts of yard size. There are a few side roads with houses, in areas where the terrain allows.

The main road includes a portion about three hundred yards long which has been cut through the base of an almost vertical cliff, barely leaving room for a narrow road shoulder and consequently barren of development. This land feature effectively divides Main Harbour into two sections. The section closer to the fishing grounds of Northern Bay and right at the end of the road consists of older houses clustered around the road and spreading out from that part of the harbour which was originally settled. It contains the school, the Anglican Church, the government wharf, the two larger stores, and the post office. The other section has developed later, consisting of houses that generally are spaced further apart, including a number of fairly recently constructed houses and stores, and importantly containing the two fish plants which have located at the 'bottom.' For local residents, however, little significance is attached to this physical schism,[11] and all see themselves as residents of Main Harbour.

There are approximately 150 different individual houses in Main Harbour, a number which closely corresponds to the number of separate residences listed in the local phone book. Almost half house families with one of seven common local surnames, a frequent situation in outports, which traditionally have maintained patterns of community patrilocality. The predominant religious affiliation is Anglican, though a small number of adherents to the United Church are found. In 1976 the labour participation rate was 43.1 per cent and the unemployment rate was an astonishing 40 per cent (compared to respective provincial figures of 49.4 and 13.4 per cent). These figures, while depicting the lack of job opportunities endemic in outports, also unfortunately may be severely skewed by the seasonality of much of the local employment in the fish plant, fishing, or in the woods. However, it is doubtful that more recent figures would show much difference.

Community and Public Services

Main Harbour has one elementary school which teaches children from kindergarten to grade eight. High school students are taken by bus approximately thirty kilometres away to a similar-sized community for grades nine through twelve. Conversations with local teachers indicate that, at present, there is a major problem in motivating even the occasional good student to attend university, a situation that is reflected in lower rates of university attainment in Main Harbour than the rest of the province (Newfoundland and Labrador Hydro, 1980, 10).

Main Harbour has a large, modern Anglican Church built in the 1960s on a high point of land close to the government wharf, and adjacent to it is the minister's residence. The minister is also in charge of religious services in Fish Arm and another nearby community, and when he is not present at a Sunday service, local lay readers substitute. During the late 1980s, the minister and his wife and children were Americans who had served the area for a number of years and were known by everyone. Main Harbour residents can recall the ministers of the past who have spent any significant length of time there, and the position, like almost all of those filled by professionals who are also 'strangers,' has traditionally been an influential one in the community. The local chapter of the Anglican Church Women's Association is the most influential voluntary association in Main Harbour, holding weekly mixed social (card games) and business meetings. This group organizes Christmas and Easter socials, participates in religious ceremonies like funerals and Church anniversaries, spearheads charitable activities such as knitting goods for overseas people identified by the Church as needy, and occasionally organizes fund drives (usually going door-to-door) for donations for people from Main Harbour or the surrounding community deemed as needing help. The ACWA is now dominated by middle-aged and older women, a pattern which is consonant with the much wider trend towards secularization among young people in Western societies, but one which has only recently been manifested and perceived as a problem in Main Harbour.[12]

Medical and dental services make Main Harbour relatively more attractive than other communities in the region. A Department of Health Clinic with a full-time nurse is located there, and the service area has also provided a free residence for the doctor. Nevertheless, continual problems in attracting and retaining the services of a physician have led to a string of short-term appointments, frequently immigrants who have volunteered, it seems, for remote service to enhance their chances of obtaining Canadian citizenship. As one result, local citizens are reluctant to make any complaints about the level or quality of medical services available. One young woman who was made to sit and wait over an hour for the doctor to fill a prescription (frequently used medications being available right at the clinic), while the doctor apparently took inventory, remarked that she would not voice a complaint because 'any doctor is better than no doctor at all.' Dental services are provided one day per week by a dentist (also foreign-trained) who lives in a neighbouring community.

The post office is a central spot of activity for the village, especially on days when unemployment (Unemployment Insurance Commission or 'pogey'), old age, or family allowance cheques are due. In the winter especially, going down to check the mail is viewed as sufficient reason for anyone to be out and about, and a good excuse for socializing. In Fish Arm and some other nearby communities the job of running of the post office is treated as a valued local plum, but the Main Harbour post office during the late 1980s was run by a woman from another part of New-foundland who was successful in a government competition. The other major government clerical position is clerk of the town council, a position also held for most of the research period by a Newfoundlander from outside the village. The town council is a fairly recent innovation, having been in operation only since the early 1980s; the positions of mayor and councillors are elected and involve part-time commitments only.

The council has taken over responsibility for water and sewer services, local road maintenance, garbage disposal, and the regulation of develop-ment as well as the collection of some municipal taxes. Other govern-ment services include telephones (critical, judging from the number of calls many citizens of Main Harbour or Fish Arm make), CBC radio and television, hydroelectric power, and the aforementioned ferry service operating twice a week between Fish Arm and Main Harbour. Cable television service arrived in Main Harbour during the period of the research. Old-timers can often recall when the first radio, television, automobiles, and so one came into the community, events which are years behind similar developments in less isolated areas.

Only a handful of private business have their own shops or outlets in Main Harbour. First and foremost, there are two general stores, one located adjacent to the government wharf and owned by a firm whose head office is outside the village, and the other run by a local person (now retired) locate quite nearby, which also houses the provincial liquor outlet. Three smaller stores service the 'bottom' section nearer the fish plants. There is a take-out (also housing a small pinball arcade which occasionally draws a few youngsters), a gas station and a shop (which also does some auto and equipment repairs), a hardware and electrical parts shed behind the house of a local electrician, and the Club, a bar or lounge serving alcoholic beverages. In recent years, owing to the upgrading of the highroad and the increasing numbers of automobiles (especially pickup trucks), shopping trips to larger centres for groceries and other essentials have become commonplace. There are usually all-day events, since it requires about two hours of driving each way. Occasionally overnight trips incorporating stays with kin and friends from Main Harbour are also taken.

Recreational facilities are very limited. There is a small playground with a seldom-used baseball field and a cleared area near a pond for summer swimming, but little else beyond the woods and the sea. To play hockey on an artificial ice surface requires travelling nearly an hour to a different community. The dominant organized pastime is darts, with both men's and women's leagues meeting once a week in the winter. The Orange Lodge also holds weekly meetings, with the primarily older men generally playing cards and chatting.

Law Enforcement in Main Harbour

Main Harbour is located about one hundred and twenty-five kilometres from the headquarters of the RCMP detachment that serves it, a distance which takes about an hour and a half during good driving weather. The detachment is responsible for a number of small towns in the area, but there are at present only two officers who regularly patrol there. Because the police are on eight-hour shifts and the round trip takes at least three hours of constant driving under good conditions, the practice is for Main Harbour to be patrolled on the same shift as two other 'neighbouring' communities (about thirty and fifty kilometres away) on the same 'highroad,' a practice which limits the amount of proactive patrolling that can be effectively implemented.

The presence of a blue and white RCMP car in Main Harbour is a noteworthy event, and one made all the more public by the existence of only one main thoroughfare along which almost all the houses are located. The local gossip and communications networks are very efficient in transmitting information, as the following conversation reveals:

NR said that some guys would be drinking around —— Cove (at the far end of Main Harbour). If the police came in (at the near side of town), their friends or family would phone down. In the two or three minutes it would take for the police to drive down there, a phone call might already have arrived. (Field notes of an interview with YA and NR)

Though there were powerful twin-cylinder snowmobiles in the yard of the local detachment and police boats were also available, neither of the officers interviewed said that he had been given the chance to use these resources, and no respondent mentioned having been chased by an RCMP officer on a snowmobile or in a boat.

According to Constable R, at one time there had been one person assigned to police just the three villages on the (then) gravel highroad which leads to Main Harbour, but this arrangement had not resulted in better policing and was hard on the police officer involved. His comments were supported by a member of the Main Harbour council:

They used to have a Mountie station at —— [name of neighbouring town], but that was no better for us than them being stationed in Centreville. We asked for a full-time policeman here, but they said that he wouldn't be on duty twenty-four hours a day, seven days a week, so your coverage would be no better than it is now with one policeman living in ——.

Fish Arm

Historically, the *raison d'être* of Fish Arm was fishing. Records indicate that it was the site of a French fishing station as far back as 1660, and a French presence was noted until the 1850s (Smallwood, 1981), though there are no persons of French origin and no trace of French settlement today. A visit by the Anglican Bishop Edward Field at that time noted that the one (anglophone) family living there spent the summers fishing for salmon and cod and the winters sealing on nearby islands.

The fine sea resources enticed early pioneers to build homes in small coves near the mouth of an eight-kilometre-long protected inlet close to the best fishing berths, as well as along the small patch of level land near the head of the inlet. Land grants were first issued in 1905 (Gunness, 1973, 22). Table 3.2 shows the local Fish Arm population, including the outer coves, at various times over the past century or so.

In 1924 a barking mill was established, attracting many people from the outer coves to the present site of the village at the head of the inlet and providing employment until it was destroyed by fire in 1927. It was never rebuilt. Rights to the fine stand of timber in the surrounding hills have since changed hands a few times, with local operations limited to small-scale pulpwood cutting overseen by a local subcontractor in each case. In the late 1970s, even this operation was abandoned, the victim, apparently, of the lack of roads and the high cost of sea transportation (Smallwood,

TABLE 3.2
Population of Fish Arm

Year	Population
1868	59
1891	107 or 239
1901	163
1945	214
1976	303
1986	275
1994	225

Sources: 1868, 1891 from *Encyclopedia of Newfoundland*. The 239 figure is from Gunnes, 1973; 1945 from the *Rounder*, 1979:31; 1976 from Statistics Canada; 1986 estimated by the Anglican minister; 1994 figure the average estimated by several residents.

1981), thus curtailing an important source of winter employment. At present, one or two small sawmill operations exist, providing for local building needs, and, of course, local males cut and transport firewood for domestic consumption.

The viability of Fish Arm has been dependent largely on the continued strength of the fishing industry. The earlier pattern of twice-yearly visits by fish-buying and supplying ships that bartered necessities in return for salted cod was altered around 1910 (Smallwood) or 1915 (Gunness, 1973) when local merchants became middlemen, and again in the 1940s when a fresh and frozen fish processing plant from a neighbouring community (not Main Harbour) set up a branch plant and started collecting fish daily for processing outside the community. A fish processing plant was built in Fish Arm in the late 1970s (concomitant with the development of long liners); it now is operated by the dominant merchant and fish buyer in the community and provides the main source of employment, other than fishing, for Fish Arm citizens.

The *raison d'être* of Fish Arm still is fishing. Fishing is done either in small boats or long liners which return nightly, thereby limiting the distance which one can fish away from home. Though cod and salmon are the main species caught, other ground fish, capelin, squid, and crab are now important. Fishing involves a strong seasonal pattern of activity as the different species enter the waters surrounding Fish Arm. When the fishing is good, it is usual for fishermen to be out at their nets from 4:00 or 5:00 a.m. sometimes until after dark. Local fishermen are proud of the fact that cod and salmon fishing in this area are much better than in Main Harbour, though there is continuous concern about the fluctuation of catches. A significant investment is required in both equipment (different types of netting, crab traps, fuel, equipment purchase and repair, and so on) and in time for the full-time fisherman.

Community Facilities and Services

Other than the large general store, there are a few other smaller stores providing mainly groceries. Fish Arm also boasts an elementary school, church, post office, nursing station for a resident nurse, and diesel-operated power plant. At present, all Fish Arm residents live in the village itself and the smaller settlements in the outer coves have been abandoned (with the exception of a few cabins recently built for recreational purposes). The advent of gasoline boat motors (putt-putts), which made it possible to travel daily from Fish Arm to the fishing berths near the outer coves, and financial inducements offered to outer cove residents during the resettlement program hastened these settlements' demise. Interestingly, the residents of Fish Arm themselves rejected resettlement, unlike many neighbouring communities of similar size (Pollard, 1974, 8).

Physical Layout

The people of Fish Arm live in houses narrowly separated from each other in two 'bottom' areas near the ends of a very poor-grade dirt road about two and a half kilometres long, or on the narrow coastal shelf which the road follows. In some places, the high hills which surround the community rise so precipitously that there is no space for even a single house, and in one spot it was necessary to blast the road path out of the cliff. A few trucks,[13] brought in by ferry, can be seen occasionally plying the road, but the main traffic consists of all-terrain vehicles, pedestrians, and snowmobiles when the ground is snow-covered. The fish plant, major merchant and fish buyer's store, government wharf, and three-room school are all located towards the centre of the connecting road. The church, the post office, the nursing station, a few small shops, and the (Orange) Lodge are found in one of the bottoms, and a small shop and a larger merchant's store in the other. The nursing station is staffed by a resident nurse,[14] who maintains close connection, by air if necessary, to a hospital in a larger town some 130 kilometres away.

Isolation

The high, steep, and heavily forested hills completely surrounding Fish

Arm physically isolate the community even more than Main Harbour. There is no road connecting Fish Arm to any other place. Other than by sea, the only routes into and out of the village follow two small brooks which empty into Northern Bay, one at each bottom. Until shortly before the period of field work, Fish Arm residents were completely isolated during the winter months, extending usually from December through as late as June when the last of the pack ice disappears. Adventurous snow-mobilers have finally (since the mid-1980s) succeeded in finding a way through the rugged terrain into Fish Arm from Main Harbour and event-ually from other communities across the barrens, bringing an end to winter isolation. These winter paths follow the brooks mentioned above, which freeze over in winter. Indeed, now there is considerable snowmo-bile traffic, including a growing number of winter tourists who now visit the village, accompanied by local guides. Fish Arm residents, including women and children, now visit other communities or spend time at the recently constructed cabins in the winter, a feat which only a few years ago was considered too dangerous except by a few daring men. The only other mode of winter transport has been small aircraft, which are able to land on a nearby pond or on the harbour ice when it has frozen over sufficiently. As soon as spring arrives and the brooks 'break out' or break through their ice covering, land passage again becomes impossible. In summer, the most common mode of transport to and from Fish Arm is by boat, either the twice-weekly ferry or private long liner.

Law Enforcement

The policing situation in Fish Arm is significantly different from Main Harbour because of the lack of road access. The police of necessity come into the village by plane or by boat, and usually with a specific purpose: to respond to complaint, to pick up someone for some police purpose, to carry out a search for poachers, etc.

The arrival of a police officer is noted quickly by the local residents, who are always interested in the arrival of someone from the outside, making surreptitious police patrol impossible. In the summer, the police sometimes use small pontoon planes to arrive at Fish Arm. These planes land in the harbour so they are readily visible and audible. In the winter, small planes must land on the frozen harbour or on a frozen pond accessible only by a snowmobile ride up some steep trails. Helicopters can land practically anywhere there is enough open territory, and in fact a helicopter pad has been built in the community as part of a summer work program. However, no respondent reported a single case of a police officer (unlike game wardens) surreptitiously entering Fish Arm for the purposes of proactive policing.

In terms of law enforcement, Fish Arm is served by an RCMP detachment located in Ruralville, about sixty-five kilometres away in the opposite direction to Main Harbour. Ruralville is also the residence and office of the game warden in whose jurisdiction Fish Arm lies. Visits by the police or game wardens are thus relatively infrequent.

4

Crime Rates and Crime Reporting in the Outports

How much crime is there in the outports of Newfoundland, and what type of crime is it? The goal of this chapter is to provide some official statistics indicating the amount of officially reported crime in rural Newfoundland, and to critically assess the validity of these figures through a consideration of outport cultural values relating to reporting to the police, and of the social processes involved in reporting.

Amount of Crime from Official Crime Rates

On the basis of police statistics, the Atlantic region has the lowest rates of serious crime in Canada, which has lower rates than the United States (e.g., Hagan, 1984). A detailed breakdown of crime within Atlantic Canada (comprising the provinces of New Brunswick, Nova Scotia, Prince Edward Island, and Newfoundland) is provided by Kaill and Smith's tally of five-year averages of selected crimes in the region from 1977 through 1981, shown in table 4.1. Within the region, Newfoundland (along with Prince Edward Island) has notably lower overall crime rates, substantially below even the regional level.[1]

Table 4.2 shows the rates of major categories of crime for Canada, Newfoundland, and Newfoundland excluding the only city, St John's, which had a population of 160,000 or 27.6 per cent of the provincial total. Figures are calculated for 1986, the year the field work for this study was initiated.

Overall, the rates of crime in rural Newfoundland are substantially lower than in St John's, thus giving further credibility to the idea that the outports of Newfoundland are one of the safest regions in North America.

Map 4
The Atlantic Provinces of Canada

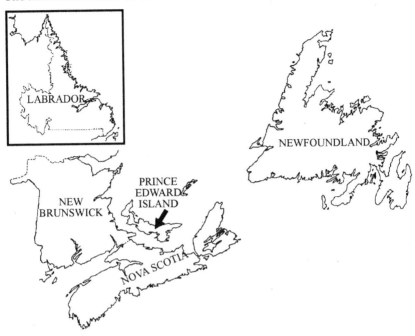

Type of Crime

Can we expect the types of crime committed in rural Newfoundland to differ from those elsewhere in Canada? Because there have been almost no studies of outport crime, or, indeed, little Canadian data on urban-rural crime differences, we turn our attention to the United States. American studies that employ police-recorded crime statistics suggest that the distribution of rural crime differs from that of urban crime. Vandalism, for example, appears to be more prevalent than larceny-theft, and there is less gang or group crime (Smith and Huff, 1982; Phillips and Wurschmidt, 1982). Other works which employ victim studies to examine urban-rural differences in crime, such as Laub's (1983),[2] which employed an American national sample, and Smith and Huff's (1982) study of a representative rural farming county in the midwestern United States, come to slightly different conclusions. They reported that patterns of victimization in rural areas were similar to those found in cities in terms of age, race, and sex, with young males being especially prone to victimization for personal

TABLE 4.1

Five-Year (1977–81) Averages of Selected Crime Statistics, Newfoundland, Atlantic Provinces, and Canada, in Rates per 100,000 Population

Crime Statistic	Nfld. and Labrador	Atlantic Provinces	(rank in Atlantic)	Canada
All criminal offences[a]	5558.1	6250.7	4	8709.8
Criminal code offences[b]	5162.6	5245.6	4	8230.3
Crimes of violence[c]	453.1	475.5	2	639.3
Property offences[d]	2952.2	3263.0	3	5341.0
Murder[e]	1.0	1.8	4	2.7
Sexual assault[f]	11.0	11.2	2	18.0
Assaults[g]	403.3	416.3	2	479.0
Vandalism[h]	961.8	1107.9	4	1244.5
All drugs/possession[i]	144.5	231.5	4	225.7
All drugs/trafficking[j]	45.5	66.7	4	52.2
Males charged, violence	153.2	165.5	3	193.8
Females charged, violence	12.9	13.0	3	19.5
Juveniles charged, violence[k]	22.5	15.6	1	36.2
Juveniles charged, vandalism	91.5	61.6	1	63.0
Juveniles charged, all crime	535.4	343.8	1	410.9

Source: Kaill and Smith, 1984.

[a]Includes criminal code offences and federal statutes (e.g., Bankruptcy Act, FDA, NCA).

[b]Exclusive of drugs and criminal driving offences.

[c]Includes homicides, attempted homicides, manslaughter, sexual assaults, robberies, and all assaults.

[d]Includes all property-related crimes (B and E, thefts, frauds).

[e]Includes first- and second-degree murder, manslaughter, and infanticide.

[f]Combines data for rape and indecent assault, to conform to legislative changes.

[g]Includes wounding with intent, assault causing bodily harm, assaulting police and peace officers, and common assaults.

[h]Includes crimes involving damage to public and private property.

[i]Does not include controlled drugs, as that category combines possession and trafficking.

[j]See note 9.

[k]Ages for juveniles are seventeen in Newfoundland but sixteen in the remaining Atlantic provinces.

crime, and property crime rates about the same in all income levels. Both studies conclude that although crime rates are lower in rural areas – a finding which is not an artifact of differential reporting or judicial processing – the patterns of victimization are so similar that criminological theories and inquiries emanating from urban settings can also be applied to rural ones.

A close examination of the official crime statistics shown in tables 4.1 and 4.2 certainly supports the pattern of there being generally less crime

TABLE 4.2
Police-Recorded Crime Rates, 1986, Newfoundland and Canada

	Canada	Nfld. excl. St John's	Nfld.
Crimes of violence	639	624	801
Property crimes	2932	2143	5660
Criminal Code total	5412	4258	8901
All infractions	7544	6711	11,169

Source: *Canadian Crime Statistics 1986* (Ottawa: Ministry of Supply and Services, 1987).

in rural Newfoundland than in more urban areas. The exception seems to be in the area of violent crime, where Newfoundland's rural area rates do not seem especially low. However, we should note that research by O'Grady (summarized in chapter 8) indicates that violence statisics in Newfoundland appear to have been artificially inflated owing to changes in police policies.

Also noteworthy is the rate of violation of provincial statutes, excluding driving offences. These include technical violations, such as of hunting and game laws. For Canada as a whole, the rate of violation of provincial statutes in rural areas is about seven times the urban rate (Kaill and Smith, 1984, table 3). Given the high proportion of the population in Newfoundland that is classed as rural, one would expect a high rate of provincial statute violation, particularly as the Atlantic regional rate is substantially higher than the national average. In fact, Newfoundland's rates are easily the lowest of the four provinces, a fact which suggests that provincial variations in behaviour and in charging practices need to be considered before any conclusions can be reached.

What about official crime statistics for the research sites? A breakdown of individuals charged over a four-and-one-half-year period in the judicial district that includes Main Harbour is provided in table 4.3.[3] These data suggest that what little crime does occur and gets reported is relatively minor. By far the largest categories concern automobile traffic, accident, and parking violations, with provincial statutes except traffic following. There is a large drop-off to theft and wilful damage. These observations tally with remarks of the provincial court judge who for years has heard cases in Main Harbour:

You know, we get a lot of minor offences – drunk, disorderly. We get some assaults. Lots of driving or having liquor in the truck; people stopping, having a

TABLE 4.3
Study Area, Crimes and Convictions: Individuals Charged, 1976–1980[a]

Offence	1976	1977	1978	1979	1980[a]
Assaults	38	42	27	66	16
B, E & thefts	80	88	70	87	39
Theft M.V.	13	17	12	15	6
Theft over $200.00	22	17	28	19	4
Theft under $200.00	128	110	102	104	34
Frauds	15	38	14	8	14
Trespass at night	–	–	5	–	–
Wilful damage	89	86	114	117	31
Disturb the peace	19	16	25	22	11
Robbery	–	–	1	–	–
Offensive weapons	6	8	8	5	4
Obstruction	4	4	1	8	3
Sex offences	–	1	5	4	4
Other Criminal Code not included above	130	162	31	26	11
Drug offences	24	21	20	36	8
Federal statutes	24	16	33	14	8
Provincial statutes except traffic	64	84	93	158	114
Impaired drivers	60	57	34	55	19
Refuse breath test	6	9	14	24	8
Drive while disqualified	–	2	1	4	–
Fail to remain at accident scene	9	12	17	20	14
Dangerous driving	–	4	2	2	–
Traffic violations	1533	1782	1545	1434	746
Parking violations	85	43	241	177	164
Fatal M.V. accidents	3	2	1	4	–
Injury M.V. accidents	29	33	27	31	15
Property damage accidents	147	120	139	185	98
Totals	2528	2774	2610	2625	1371

[a]To June 1980.
Source: Newfoundland and Labrador Hydro, August 1980

drink and being ticketed by the police, impaired driving, that sort of thing. A little bit of theft and vandalism. (Field notes, interview of Judge O)

The judge said, 'Ninety per cent of the cases were liquor-related, with people getting into fights and scuffles, assaults and that sort of thing.' This included 'even sexually-related offences.' The 'run of the mill' offender was a young male eighteen or nineteen years of age, and, in the judge's memory, no female offender from Main Harbour had ever appeared before him.

One of the police officers who patrolled the area held a similar view of the crime problem. There was 'a little bit of vandalism and a little bit of theft, some driving offences – nothing major' (field notes, interview of Constable T). In fact, people in the Main Harbour area were so nice, friendly, and co-operative with the police that an officer who had for years been posted here 'just loved it.'

In summary, the official, police-recorded statistics and the impressions of local criminal justice officials paint a very rosy picture of rural New-foundland, the category which includes all of the outports. It appears that the outports have very low crime rates, and those crimes that are reported tend to be mundane and minor in nature. If there is an anomaly, the outports exhibit slightly higher rates of crimes of violence than expected, and exceptionally low rates of violations of provincial statutes. The official statistics certainly support a view of the outports as perhaps the safest region in North America.

The Problem of Crime Reporting

Police-recorded crime rates have been severely criticized as a basis for inferring actual crime rates. Large-scale national studies of victims in the United States conducted annually since the early 1970s (see Waller and Okihiro, 1978; Smith and Huff, 1982, 272 for brief descriptions) and Canadian studies by Koenig (1974), Waller and Okihiro (1978), Klein et al. (1978), and the Canadian Urban Victimization Survey (Solicitor-General of Canada, 1983) and the General Social Survey (Gartner and Doob, 1996) all report that a large proportion of the population does not report crime. Typical reasons include the victim's judging the incident insufficiently serious, believing that 'the police couldn't do anything about it anyway,' or feeling that reporting is an 'inconvenience,' or the fact that nothing was taken or the items were returned, or that the crime was a 'personal matter' (Solicitor-General of Canada, 1984).

There are two general reasons for being particulary suspicious of crime rates in the outports of Newfoundland. First, as we saw in the last chapter, the outports have been almost totally neglected in terms of law enforcement services provided by governments both before and after Confederation. Not only that, the administration of justice has historically been partisan and unfair to most outport residents, who generally have had little or no effective say in or control over the outside institutions that have imposed rules and regulations. Under these conditions, it is not unreasonable to assume that there may be an increased cultural reluctance to involve the police or other outside enforcement officials when a crime occurs.

The second line of reasoning relates to research on citizen experiences with and attitudes towards the police. A number of studies indicate that most contact with the police is citizen-initiated, with the police playing a reactive, as opposed to proactive, role (e.g., review by Hagan, 1984). When the police respond to a citizen request and provide an instrumental service such as apprehending a criminal, directing traffic, or making a report for insurance purposes (cf. Waller and Okihiro, 1978), satisfaction tends to be high. Indeed, levels of satisfaction with the police seem to be high in places like Toronto (Courtis and Dessuyer, 1970) and in Canada as a whole (see review by Griffiths, and Verdun-Jones, 1994, 89–90). However, when the police engage in proactive activity such as enforcing speed limits and other technical regulations, citizen hostility is common (see Ericson, 1982; Wiley and Hudik, 1974). Inasmuch as rural fishing villages in Atlantic Canada are not favoured with a constant police presence and it is not possible for the police to function as a twenty-four-hour social service agency (cf. Griffiths et al., 1980), and inasmuch as police contact is likely to be of the proactive type, attitudes towards the police are likely to be less positive, and thus one would expect lower reporting patterns.

Perceptions of the Police in the Outports

How do residents of Main Harbour and Fish Arm view law enforcement officials? One of the most noteworthy features of Main Harbour and Fish Arm life for me was the way in which outside professionals holding official positions of power are treated: they are accorded a degree of deference and respect that in many cases shades over into outright fear. The minister, the doctor or resident nurse, and the police officer are recipients and beneficiaries of this phenomenon.

The general fear of and deference to the police seem to be island-wide. For example, Widdowson's (1977) study of images and legends used in the verbal social control of Newfoundland children reports that the police and the Mounties are generally treated as threatening and frightening strangers, often employed to coerce children into suitable behaviour. The accounts in this section of the chapter suggest that attitudes towards the police in the outports are different from those held by most Canadians.

These attitudes mean that reporting to the police is more unlikely in the outports than almost anywhere else, and thus the validity of outport crime statistics based on police records is doubtful.

In the remote outports studied, police visits are fairly rare, especially to Fish Arm. This is clearly a function of the cost in both time and money of travel to these isolated villages. A trip to Main Harbour by police car involves a whole day of travel, often on dangerous roads, while a trip to Fish Arm might involve two days by boat or an expensive helicopter or aircraft flight. Because of the cost factors, police officers do not have the luxury of making a routine patrol or engaging in community services that bolster their image among the public. As one RCMP officer explained, he barely has enough time on a shift to drive to Main Harbour, look after whatever complaints he has, and return to the detachment headquarters. This officer indicated that even if he happened to be in the Main Harbour area, he did not stop at any of the stores or the Club, but simply drove down to the end of the town and turned around. If he saw something illegal, he would act on it right away, but otherwise he just relied on complaints (field notes, interview of Officer M).

In both Main Harbour and Fish Arm, many incidents of police-citizen contact involved police attempts to track down illegal hunting, particularly poaching of moose and, to a lesser extent, caribou. One such incident, which occurred several years prior to the beginning of the field work, involved a massive search of many houses in Fish Arm by RCMP officers, accompanied by provincial game wardens. On this particular occasion, two helicopters were used to bring in the law enforcement officers, who then conducted a house-to-house search for contraband meat while the helicopters were kept flying to observe the movements of everyone in the village. The reaction of SA, a fisherman who, like most of the others, had some illegally obtained moose meat in his refrigerator (freezer) was typical:

He said that at that time he didn't know what to do ... he took the quarters (of moose) and hid them in the attic. In getting to the attic, though, he scraped his sides because it was so narrow. When the Mounties had left, not having found any meat, SA and his wife kept some to cook and they threw the rest (away) in the snow. Two days later the Mounties came back again. SA and his wife didn't know what to do about the (illegal) meat they still had in the pot. He said, 'Well, that finished me with moose. If I ever get out of this, I'll never do that again.'

Such cavalier searches of an entire village by law enforcement officials were fairly common even in the 1980s in Fish Arm. The unquestioning acceptance of this police practice indicates the deference towards authority and the powerlessness felt by the majority of residents. When asked why the people appeared to be so afraid of the police, SA replied, 'Well, everyone had meat back then.' There was no mention of requesting a search warrant or challenging the authority of officials.

Several people recounted the same story about HM, who was so frightened of the Mounties that, when they came to her door to inquire about a problem of roving dogs, she just stuttered 'Yes' to all their questions. As one villager jokingly put it, 'I suppose, if the Mountie asked can I take you into the bedroom she would have said yes.'[4]

A highly unusual local reaction to a situation of confrontation with the police was that of a fisherman who was known for his fearless demeanour. The game warden (accompanied by police) wanted to search the house, but was prevented from doing so by the fisherman, who stood outside his locked door and refused get out of the way when the game warden requested him to do so. A brief scuffle took place, but the game warden did not succeed in gaining entry. This event became locally celebrated and noteworthy because it indicated a lack of fear and submission that was exceptional.

Police Visits as Trouble

Because the community is so isolated and police contact so infrequent, a visit by the police into the community of Fish Arm invariably spells trouble for someone. Even in Main Harbour, where police patrol by automobile is possible, the arrival of the police usually means trouble. A perhaps typical example was related by a friend of two young Main Harbour adults who were engaged in a common outport practice: drinking in public.

A couple of guys, WM and DI, were parked at the side of the road and drinking in a pickup truck went the cops came by. Thinking quickly, DI dumped his bear into the cab of the truck, but WM didn't and was caught with an open bottle of beer and was charged. DI wasn't charged with drinking but the cops wanted to take him in for a breathalyser test. He said he wanted to go home first and tell his wife that he had to go to Centreville with the police, but the police wouldn't let him do that. So, DI said he wouldn't go in and he was charged with refusing a breathalyser test. (Field notes)

In the outports where face-to-face communication is the norm, the attitudes towards the police held by individual citizens are partly a function of past relationships with individual officers. There has only been a handful of Mounties who have patrolled Main Harbour, and something of their policing style and personality quickly becomes known:

PL said that once in a while they got a Mountie, usually a young one who was out to make arrests. He gave the example of the Mountie named Y, who was always after the kids for drinking. The kids really felt that this cop was breathing down their necks. They used to play games with him, trying to get him to chase them. Every once in a while, one would get caught, however.

Another villager, in commenting on this same officer Y, suggested that he was 'looking for a promotion.' This officer was the exception, however; most who have had contact in the area were more 'laid back,' since there was not much (crime) going on here anyway.

The Social Calculus of Reporting

Throughout the research period, a number of individuals described incidents of criminal behaviour that occurred both recently and decades ago. Because of the isolation of these outports and the visibility of strangers, in almost every case, the perpetrator or perpetrators are members of the community. It has been an easy matter to track down the culprits because everyone has intimate knowledge of everyone else's behaviour patterns and possessions. Anything out of the ordinary, such as different items of dress or spending money in local stores, is likely to be commented upon. In one case in Main Harbour, for example, three youths broke into a store, took liquor and cigarettes, and then stole a boat, rowed across the bay, and tried to sell the goods there. A suspicious merchant of that community phoned a store owner in Main Harbour, who then called a number of other businesses and thus found out about the crime.

When the offenders are local, reporting the incident to the police is tantamount to getting a neighbour in trouble. In such circumstances, many choose not to report at all. Thus, the owner of the largest general store in Main Harbour related:

'I had some cans of tar out beside the shed over where we store the liquor now. Well, someone came along that night and put holes in them. There was sticky tar all over the place. What a mess! Well, I just asked around and found out who did it. I didn't phone the police. I told them to pay for it or I would call the police, and they always did pay for it. ... If I phone the police, the next night I could find the front of the store tore off, or someone could throw a few stones through the windows of the store.' (Field notes, interview of GK)

Probably a larger concern for the merchant whose market is the local area is the impact on business of reporting incidents. The following field notes relate a conversation with a manager of the Club in Main Harbour:

He said, 'The only problem we have is people treating the pinball machines and the pool table rough. How I deal with that is I talk to them the next day.' I asked him what he said and he said that he tells them that if they keep that up he'll have to bar them. He emphasized that 'you have to treat people pretty good around here: there's not that many customers and if you treat them bad you won't have any business.' (Field notes, LT)

In a similar vein, PL, the proprietor of another small store, indicated that theft was minor but that 'it was a problem you've always got to worry about.' He gave an example of a local man who came into the store and asked for something that could be used for a chafing sore on his legs. PL suggested Solarcaine, noting there was only one tube of it left in the store. The customer left some time later without having paid for it. The store owner and his helper thought the customer might have decided not to take it and had put it down somewhere, but a thorough search did not turn up the tube. Asked why he never brought up the incident with the customer or reported it to the police, PL reasoned that 'he'd probably say that he paid for it or didn't take it,' and that 'it would just cause bad feelings and [I'm] not going to get anything back anyhow.'

There were many incidents of personal victimization which were not reported.

RI related an event that occurred in Fish Arm, in which she and SL were victims. She said that they were going to church on a Sunday night. From the hill behind their house in Fish Arm, you could see everything that they were doing. Whoever it was that robbed them (and they had their suspicions) was probably watching. At any rate, when they went to church, SL apparently forgot to close the trap door in the bottom of the house. When they came back, RI noticed that her bedspread was untidy and then knew that someone had been in the home. When she checked her purse in the bureau drawer, she found that $150 that she had put there was missing and that the drawers in her bureau were also disarrayed.

Then she went down to tell SL to check his money. SL had hidden $200 underneath a bible, which he said was not a very obvious place to search, but the money was missing. They never called the police. When they told neighbours what had happened, they said the neighbours didn't believe them because they didn't believe that SL or RI had that much money around – money being a scarce commodity at that time. As I mentioned before, they had their suspicions and were convinced that SU, a neighbour who had visited earlier in the day, had done it. According to RI, 'it's the ones who come around and see what you have who are the ones who steal.' At any rate, the money was never returned. But RI noted that three weeks later she got a phone call from a distraught neighbour saying that her place had been robbed as well. (Field notes, RI)

Firestone (1967) and Faris (1973) have extensively described the ritualistic patterns of behaviour resulting from the need to maintain social harmony and peace in the outports, where people have historically been isolated and reliant upon each other for survival and where there is little formal authority. In the culture of the outports, even *verbal* aggression is sanctioned (cf. Faris, 1973; Szwed, 1966, ch. 5). Similarly, it is usual for people in Main Harbour and Fish Arm to hint indirectly when they want someone else to perform a service, even something as trivial as getting a ride to the post office. A direct request puts social pressure on the individual to agree, in addition to obligating the requester to reciprocate in a socially acceptable fashion some time in the future. Thus, for people who are members of what Faris (1973) calls the 'moral community of the outport,' reporting another member to the police is an act of interpersonal aggression that can have severe social consequences. For example, one Main Harbour resident commented, 'There's a lot of people who don't report to the police. If it's a neighbour or a neighbour's kid, well, in a little place like this everyone belongs to the same organizations. If you report your neighbour, you'll see him at a meeting later and you'll have to give him the "cold shoulder."'

Avoidance and Immunity to Sanctions for Reporting

One way of getting around the moral dilemma associated with calling the police while still maintaining some semblance of solidarity is to report an incident immediately, before the offender is known. The act of reporting thus has an impersonal quality. One respondent who had his snowmobile stolen phoned the police as soon as he was unable to locate it, before he knew who had taken it. Finding the offender was an easy task for the police because the machine was stolen at night close to the Club and the list of suspects boiled down to the late drinkers at the Club. Ultimately, however, the victim did not press charges when the police came, but instead agreed to have the offender pay for damage done to the snowmobile.

Some members of the moral community are more immune to social sanctioning than others and thus are freer to report to the police or involve outside agencies. The family of the owner of the major business in Fish Arm fits this category. One respondent blamed his being summonsed to court for supplying liquor to minors – perhaps not an unusual behaviour, since it is easy to observe minors drinking and even with drinking problems – on the fact that one of his close relatives had recently 'had a row' or serious disagreement with this merchant. This same person was also convinced that an episode that resulted in his conviction for drinking in public was reported by someone in the dominant merchant's family who phoned the police because of comments made to the merchant's wife by a group of young people who were drinking with the respondent on the public dock. However, because of the businessman's economic hold on the community, little effective retaliatory action was taken for reporting to the police.

The reluctance to call the police is especially evident when dramatic violations of social order occur. One noteworthy case involved a man who, apparently motivated by a belief in the unfaithfulness of his wife, tied her to a bed, burned her clothes, and beat her. Rather than the police, the resident minister was called upon to take action. This resulted in the wife and children being placed in a home away from the area and the husband eventually being put in a mental hospital. Only when the behaviour became intolerable was the norm of non-aggression superseded and action taken, and even then the police were not involved.

Immunity to social sanctioning for reporting someone is available to the person who calls police anonymously. The advent of publicized hot lines to law enforcement agencies (see chapter 5 for an analysis of the effect of the 'poacher' hot line) has increased reporting of even minor crime. When such anonymous reporting occurs, inevitably there is extended discussion of who reported, and why. Such behaviour, of course, increases the level of suspicion and distrust in small, tightly knit communities.

KW was of the opinion that someone must have had it in for his relative for the relative's place to be searched for poached meat by the police. A long discussion among the four men present took place, with much of the time spent trying to figure out who the informer might have been. KW said he thought the reason his relative was reported had to do with personalities. He said that he himself was the 'prime pusher' of moose meat in these parts and everyone knew it, but he was also the kind of person who would say hello to anyone, and as a result, everyone, even those in Centreville and —— (name of another large town), knew him. His relative, on the other hand, was grouchy and so probably someone reported him.

The social sanctions against crime and against calling the police have less effect on those who are not full members of the moral community. In Main Harbour, much of the local crime has been blamed on two or three specific youths who have jail records. Because of their reputations as troublemakers, phoning the police when another crime involving them has taken place does not seem to incur social punishment. Had these youths been part of a family that 'belonged to' Main Harbour and did not have a criminal reputation, a different course of action likely would have been taken. These particular youths occupied a marginal position in the moral community from the start in that their families had recently moved to Main Harbour to take employment in the fish plants. The general community disapproval of them was readily expressed. Thus NE, a teenaged respondent, observed that one of them was really lazy (a very negative attribute in this community) and 'wouldn't be liking the fact that he would be put to work clearing trees' while in jail. Another was seen as deceitful: 'He was the nicest kind of guy. He'd do anything for you. If you wanted something from him, he'd give it to you with a smile on his face, but at the same time, he goes around stealing. That's not the kind of person I want to hang around with' (field notes, OF).

Conclusion

In this chapter, official crime rate figures have been presented which portray the outports of Newfoundland as one of the safest regions in North America, a region where what crime does occur tends to be relatively minor in nature. While not disputing the main thrust of the view that the outports are indeed safe places, the main argument of this chapter is that these crime statistics need to be understood in the specific cultural and policing context of the outports. There is undoubtedly more crime than official records indicate because inhabitants have come to view police as threatening outsiders whose visits result in trouble for someone known. Reporting also violates cultural norms of non-aggression that have emerged in the outports, norms which are especially effective in isolated and intimate communities where offenders, victims, and witnesses are generally neighbours for a lifetime.

This does not mean, however, that the low rates of crime found in Newfoundland are entirely an artifact of low reporting. The informal social sanctions found in the outport have historically been very effective in controlling not only reporting patterns, but criminal behaviour itself.

5

Patterns of Outport
Big Game Poaching

This chapter examines the practice of illegal hunting of game animals, especially moose and caribou. Big game poaching as a crime in the outports is of particular significance because it is perhaps the most visible manifestation of the process of cultural conflict and change that is occurring with alarming speed in fishing and forestry-based communities in Newfoundland and other parts of Atlantic Canada in the throes of modernization. As indicated in chapters 1 and 2, hunting for the table was a necessary economic activity that was part of the traditional way of life in outport communities. Because of this and because the economic situation for most outport citizens still requires a flexible optimization of sources of economic support, community cultural norms still support subsistence hunting. Hunting, legal or not, is an activity which a great number of able-bodied men of the outports engage in. However, government rules and regulations concerning the hunt have proliferated and have been implemented through a sophisticated law enforcement effort and increasingly severe punishment meted out to those caught. The conflict between community norms and state regulations has made poaching an important regional crime issue.

The goal of this chapter is to present a current description of big game poaching activity and to attempt to explain the peculiar patterns of behaviour observed as an adaptation to a number of forces impinging on the actors. First, the way in which committed hunters carry out their activity has been strongly influenced by law enforcement practices designed to thwart poaching, and be sentencing practices which punish perpetrators with increasing effectiveness and harshness. Some background information on the development of game laws and their present enforcement is thus provided. The bulk of the chapter describes the nature of outport poaching as it is affected by popular sentiments surrounding hunting and by the relations and tensions among neighbours in small, isolated outports where it is often difficult to hide one's behaviour.

Academic Treatment of Big Game Poaching

There has been precious little study by criminologists of big game poaching. The major criminological interest focuses on the political aspects surrounding the passage of hunting regulations (e.g., Thompson, 1975; Thomas, 1983; Overton, 1980; McGrath, n.d. #1; McGrath, 1992). For example, Thompson's study focused on the Black Act of 1723 in England, which began the process of usurping peasants' hunting rights by the wealthy and powerful who wanted to retain game for their own recreation. Overton's thesis that the development of laws regulating the hunting of caribou in Newfoundland was the result of pressure by interest groups desiring the preservation of game as a tourist resource is described later in this chapter.

Brymer (1990) has produced a typology of hunting that is relevant to the description of outport poaching. His category of 'local rural hunter' represents a group of traditional hunters who are hold-overs from a pre-industrial agrarian communal/familial network. With the imposition of game laws, their activities became illegal, thus producing a deviant subculture among those who continued hunting. This subculture is marked by perceptions of a traditional right to hunt in the hunting 'territory,' the use of the game for food or other instrumental purposes, and the sharing of game within social networks. Brymer's category of local rural hunter is believed to fit the case of poor southern whites, marginal ranchers of western Canada and the United States, marginal farmers of northern Ontario, Quebec, and the Maritimes, and marginal fishermen of the Maritimes.[1] His description of his own and his extended family's hunting experiences in an American rural area points to many parallels with the present research.

Another recent unpublished paper, this one by McGrath (n.d #2), describes illegal hunting activity on the Avalon Peninsula, and, like Brymer's study, was undertaken with members of his own family. The illegal hunting in that area is carried out using all-terrain vehicles. Among the family unit studied, hunting successfully was a prestige-conferring activity and a constant topic of conversation and solidarity among the males who did it. For this group, getting a licence to hunt big game was necessary to justify one's presence in the woods with a firearm, but once one's presence was legitimized, a myriad of ways of violating the regulations of a big game licence were employed. As opportunists, they usually took any chance to kill an animal, with the threat of being caught seen as part of the game and necessitating a number of adaptations. The hunters did not see themselves as poachers because they used the animals for food. McGrath's description of hunting on all-terrain vehicles appears similar to the description of hunting specifics offered in Mandville's (1974) unpublished interview of a hunter from Newfoundland's south coast. The patterns of poaching reported in this chapter and in chapter 6 derive from descriptions of winter big game poaching on the northeast coast of Newfoundland in two different communities, using information from a number of sources, and thus are more likely to represent typical patterns than either McGrath's or Brymer's study.

The Development of the Newfoundland Game Laws

The emergence of the mercantile or 'truck' or 'credit' system in the Newfoundland fishery during the latter part of the nineteenth and the early part of the twentieth century was described in chapter 2. While serving to buffer the individual fisherman from the vagaries of the world fish market, the system was extremely exploitive and kept fishermen impoverished. In this context, many families were forced to accept government relief or local work when available, and to engage in subsistence activities such as farming, collecting fruits and berries, cutting wood for fuel, and making handicrafts, in order to survive. The hunting of woodland caribou and the small number of deer that were native to the island of Newfoundland was an important element of the 'traditional' economy, providing food for the consumption of those living at the subsistence level as well as articles of commerce (McGrath, 1992, 68; Overton, 1980, 1).

The practice during the 1800s was for fishermen to go by boat along rivers and inlets, and then by foot to the interior, and camp out on main caribou migration paths where the animals would be trapped, caught in pits, or shot, often while crossing water, and the skins and meat transported back to settlements. In other areas, the hunting occurred in January when the ground was frozen and dog teams could be used to transport the meat to the coast (Overton, 1980). The first legislation in Newfoundland dealing with the caribou recognized their importance as a food source by making it unlawful 'wantonly to shoot, kill or destroy them except for the purpose of food or sale and a penalty for breaking the law was imposed' (Overton, 1980, unnumbered).

By the late 1800s, the limits of the traditional salt cod fishery were reached as a source of employment and the government was searching for alternative sources of employment and industry. The increasing access to the caribou made possible by the completion of the trans-Island railway, the increasing population of outport settlement, and the practice of using the caribou to feed workers in the new mining, forestry, telegraph, and railway projects, put a severe strain on the caribou resource.

From 1879 to the early 1900s a series of legislative measures was passed that were aimed at obtaining maximum economic benefits from the caribou, which in practice meant the support of sports hunting for tourists and the loss of rights for poor settlers. The use of pits, falls, traps, dogs, and snares was outlawed, eventually making the use of a rifle the only way to kill deer (Overton, 1980, unnumbered). In addition, closed seasons and bag limits were introduced, along with licence requirements. The rights of poor settlers to kill deer in the closed season were originally written into the laws, but this practice declined over time. Local magistrates could find a person not guilty if there was 'dire need.'

The reduced numbers of the caribou in this period precipitated the introduction of the moose as a food source in 1878 and 1904 (Mercer and Manuel, 1974, 657). With no major browsing competitors, the moose have multiplied, unchecked except for human exploitation. As early as the 1930s, moose had become a staple of the outport diet (McGrath, 1992, 69). Shortly before the study there were an estimated seventy thousand animals in the province. Owing to restrictive regulations on hunting caribou, their population has recovered to an estimated forty thousand (Newfoundland and Labrador Wildlife Division, 1985, 2).

Moose regulations appear to have followed a pattern similar to caribou regulations, beginning with bull-only seasons in 1945, the development of a zone system in 1953 to regulate harvest according to moose densities, and the subsequent institution of closed seasons, quota systems, and licensing limitations on a zonal basis. In the early 1980s the provincial government, concerned about a decrease in the moose population attributed to illegal hunting, initiated a 'war' against poachers. In his seminal analysis of the reasons why poaching, a crime for 150 years, suddenly emerged as a major social issue, McGrath (1992) points to the provincial government's desire to expand the outdoor tourist industry and to reserve big game to non-resident hunters as crucial factors. This resulted in harsher penalties for those caught, a reduction in the number of moose-hunting licences, the introduction of a hunter education and safety program, and the establishment of Operation SPORT (*Stop POach-*

ing *Report Today*), a toll-free twenty-four-hour-a-day 'hot line' to allow anonymous reporting of poachers (cf. McGrath n.d. #2, unnumbered). These arrangements were in place at the time I entered the field.[2]

In 1986–7, the first year of the field work for this study, a total of 12,440 moose licences and 1865 caribou licences were available for the fall hunt (Newfoundland and Labrador Wildlife Division, 1986–7, 2), while about thirty-thousand applications (representing some sixty thousand persons) were received in 1984 (Newfoundland and Labrador Wildlife Division, 1985, 4), indicating a large discrepancy between those desiring a moose licence and those receiving one. Licensees are required to pass a hunter capability test, are restricted in regard to times, type and calibre of ammunition, and the use of dogs or vehicles, and are required to tag each quarter and surrender the lower jawbone of the moose or caribou to the Wildlife Division (Newfoundland and Labrador Wildlife Division, 1986–7).

The Development of the Game Law Enforcement Structure

With the development of laws regulating the hunting of the caribou for the use of outport residents, a Game Protection Society was set up in the 1890s which employed its own 'watchers' to enforce the laws and to press for protection of the caribou from slaughter by settlers or hunters. In 1902 these watchers became employees of the Department of Marine and Fisheries, and in 1910 a more extensive system of wardens was set up under the auspices of a Game and Inland Fisheries Board (Overton, 1980, unnumbered). The lack of funds, the employees' part-time status, and the recruitment of wardens from the local population and their consequent reluctance to apprehend friends and relatives all contributed to the continuing ineffectiveness of enforcement and the decline of the caribou herds. By 1930 estimates of the number of caribou on the Island ranged from two hundred to two thousand, a very small fraction of the forty to two hundred and fifty thousand estimated to live on the Island at the turn of the century (Overton, 1980, unnumbered).

As noted above and in chapter 2, the financial problems of the Newfoundland government prior to the Depression precluded significant expansion of the game enforcement apparatus. The Commission of Government was also very prudent financially, though it is clear that a large part of the mandate of the Newfoundland Rangers included enforcement of the game laws. With Confederation, enforcement of the game regulations was put under the umbrella of the provincial Ministry of Mines and Resources, and within the ministry, in the charge of a deputy minister responsible for both a Wildlife Division and a Forestry Division. The field staff, consisting of full-time inspectors responsible for assigned districts, full-time wardens, and half-time employees who spent the other half-year working with the Dominion Fisheries Service, worked in a dual capacity in forestry and game work (Wildlife Management Institute, 1955, 6).

As a result of a study commissioned by the government, recommendations were made for the creation of a separate Wildlife Division and, in the area of enforcement, for a few well-trained men who could co-operate with other law enforcement agencies such as the RCMP, rather than a great number of untrained individuals (Wildlife Management Institute, 1955).

The current enforcement of hunting regulations is the responsibility of the Wildlife Division of the provincial Ministry of Culture, Recreation and Sport. Under the provision of the Wild Life Act (1970 with many amendments), wildlife officers have extensive powers of search, arrest without warrant, and seizure and confiscation.[3] The arsenal of the Wildlife Division employed in the study area in the winter included aerial surveillance in small fixed-wing aircraft and helicopters, ground patrols by game wardens on snowmobiles, and occasionally extensive house searches for contraband meat often involving the RCMP as backup units.[4] Patrol by aircraft or helicopter is extremely effective in good weather, as indicated by field notes from an interview with the wildlife supervisor for the Main Harbour area:

With the helicopter up there, there's no place in Newfoundland where the trees are so thick that you can't see the ground. What they do is look for snowmobile tracks and follow them, or look for human tracks made by rackets or something else. Usually they can tell from where the tracks lead and from the pattern of tracks whether they are following animals or not, and whether a kill has taken place. Apparently, there's not a lot of difficulty in doing that.

Ground patrols are done by wildlife officers who, in winter, snowmobile in the uninhabited country, often alone. They occasionally base their operations in remote cabins erected for that purpose. These officers are on call twenty-four hours a day, seven days a week, allowing them autonomy in chasing down poachers. Their hours are kept track or by diaries and logs (interview with wildlife supervisor).

The two communities that were the subject of this study were served by wildlife officers (sometimes referred to as game wardens, a class of wildlife officer) from two separate district offices, and they, along with occasional backup by RCMP officers, were the sole contact most people had with the Wildlife Department. The game wardens, unlike the RCMP, are recruited from the local population and are, or become, well known to most people in the isolated outports.

The Social Distribution of Poaching

Illegal hunting is an activity that requires a good deal of knowledge and experience. In this part of Newfoundland, big game hunting, legal or illegal, is primarily a winter activity which involves the use of snowmobiles, though there is a regulated fall hunt as well. The hunting itself generally takes place either in the woods or in open areas a significant distance from any populated area and often in overcast or snowy conditions ('dirty' weather) so as to avoid aerial surveillance by the Wildlife Department. The dangers of going into uninhabited country where help may be miles away, the possibility of getting lost or having to wait out a storm, the severe exertion of running after a moose on rackets, the heavy work involved in butchering and carrying out the carcasses, and the exertion of snowmobiling in hilly terrain all result in hunting being seen and carried out primarily as an activity of able-bodied males. Few active big game poachers in Main Harbour or Fish Arm are over age fifty or so, and few are under age eighteen, the legal age requirement for obtaining a big game licence.

Big game hunting, legal or illegal, is an activity that requires at least one partner. The selection of partners for hunting generally seems to follow lines of peer friendship, mutual interest, and mutual trust, the individuals often having grown up with each other. Partners are frequently related through blood or marriage. One respondent, UA, who admitted that he poached a little, said that 'normally two or four guys, usually four guys, go in the woods and they get out and get a quarter (of the carcass) each' (field notes). It is not always the case, however, that close friends go hunting. Respondent DB, a person who had developed a reputation for successful hunting, relayed an incident when he was asked by a person who had never gone in the woods poaching before to accompany him and two others to get a moose 'because he was doing it for everyone else, so why not us.' When DB objected that he did not have enough gas in his 'machine' (snowmobile), he was told that they already had his tank filled and his lunch packed. With no legitimate excuse left, he left early the next morning with them and shot a moose. At the other extreme, a fisherman in his fifties who had done a lot of hunting in his youth in Fish Arm, but who was now living in Main Harbour, admitted that he had not been hunting for the last couple of years. He said 'I guess it would be better to apply [for a moose licence] if you had someone to go in the woods with.'

Poaching does not seem to be limited to 'poor settlers' or those who are needy. Those who have been actually charged with poaching include a member of a dominant merchant family in Fish Arm, a fisherman with enough financial substance to charter a plane and fly in a brand new snowmobile within hours of his old one being confiscated by the game wardens, and an employee with a provincial utility company. Prominent citizens of both communities either admitted to being, or were indicated by respondents as being, people who either were now engaged in poaching or had engaged in poaching in the past. However, those who were most heavily involved in poaching by necessity spent a lot of time in the woods, often in secluded cabins, and were for the most part economically and socially marginal in the community. Respondent KW, for example, a logger who worked outside the region during the week, called himself a 'prime pusher' of moose meat and spent practically every weekend in outdoors activity around the cabin he shared with others. He subsequently built his own cabin. Respondent LE was a shareman[5] on a long liner who collected unemployment insurance benefits in the winter and had a lot of disposable time for 'going in the country.'

Community Sentiments concerning Poaching

Given the long history of exploitation, impoverishment, and subsistence survival in the outports of Newfoundland, it should be no surprise that community norms and mores in regard to hunting emphasize its importance as a food source more than its illegality. The isolation of the outports has long placed a premium on the ability to support one's family without outside help. A number of respondents indicated that in the past, hunting was a necessity and there was nothing wrong with a person who killed a moose to feed his family. An older, retired shareman, for example, related the story of a family that, with eleven children to feed, moved to an isolated cove some miles up the coast and 'came back fatter than they ever were because there was all kinds of caribou up there' (field notes, SL). This was seen as the best possible thing the head of the family could do under the circumstances.

A person who worked seasonally at the fish plant and was a part-time fisherman indicated that most of the meat his family consumed during the winter came from hunting, legal and illegal, of moose, caribou, seal, and rabbits. He estimated spending only about $15.00 on store-bought meat over this period, mostly on chicken so as to get a bit more variety in the family diet.[6]

Studies of the outport household economy all support the idea that hunting provides a significant economic contribution to outport families. In an extended analysis of earlier figures, Brox (1972, 10) estimated that non-cash contributions to the family budget, including housing, produced benefits that were one and a half times the value of cash income from wages and sales. Hunting contributed $140.00 or one-fifth of the non-cash income in a hypothetical Bonavista family, out of a total budget of just less than $5000 (Dyke, 1966, cited in Brox, 1972). Ames' (1977) study of the importance of hunting in northern Labrador provides a more recent analysis of the economic importance of hunting in an isolated community. Likewise, in his study of George, an unemployed outport male, Wadel (1986, 66) indicates that more than four hundred pounds of 'fresh' (as opposed to the frozen meats) that George got to share from a successful legal moose hunt meant a lot to 'a big crowd like mine.'

Part of the reason for community support of hunting and trapping for the table is the lack of attractive and affordable alternatives. The small stores that serve the communities frequently have a small and expensive selection. People complain the meat and fruits and vegetables available in local stores are of poor quality, often rotting and generally not fit to buy (cf. Ames, 1977). Indeed, some Main Harbour residents make weekly trips to a larger town, Centreville, in order to shop for better-quality groceries at more reasonable prices.

Sentiments supportive of poaching for economic reasons are now held by many individuals. One Main Harbour respondent, a respected fisherman, said:

'I have nothing against poaching. I'm not ashamed of it. Everybody around here poaches. If you went down and looked at their refrigerators [freezers] here, 90 per cent of the people would have poached meat. It saves quite a bit on the grocery bills.' (Field notes)

A Fish Arm man provided similar information:

If a man goes out and gets a moose for his family, there's nothing wrong with

that, even it is illegal. At one time that was all they had to do to get their meat
– that was all they had. (Field notes)

The general community approval of poaching when the meat is used for
local consumption is partly because a fairly wide circle of kin and friends
are likely to share in the spoils. Such people, and sometimes others who,
for various reasons, are unable to obtain game themselves, can expect to
get a 'meal' or two from a moose, a fact that is partly the result of extensive kinship networks found in the communities (cf. Brymer, 1990). One
woman who is a stalwart church member and esteemed homemaker,
probably the last person one would suspect of possession of illegal meat
in an urban setting, expressed great glee at having received a meal of
moose meat from her brother, who had got it from another relative.
Another indication of the community support for poaching for local
consumption was the report that 'one fellow had a wedding a while back
where they served moose.' The informant noted that this public serving
(since practically everyone in the community was invited to set down at
the wedding meal) of moose meat did not result in charges, in spite of
the general knowledge that the meat was illegally obtained.

Successful hunting, whether legal or illegal, requires characteristics and
traits which are highly valued in the outports. Two people originally from
a small outer cove described the considerable respect felt for the leader
of a successful hunting operation in the days before snowmobiles were
used. His success involved 'being good in the woods' as well as significant
organizing ability, as the leader was the person responsible for position-
ing men in such a way that the greatest number of animals would be
killed without the five or six men involved shooting each other. In this
particular case, the leaser was referred to with the prefix 'Uncle,' denoting positive regard.

Hunting and poaching are also esteemed because proficiency requires
hard work, endurance, and physical toughness. There were a number of
instances where these outport values were made explicit. One very successful Main Harbour fisherman related his extensive work history and
attributed his success directly to his ability to work long and hard at difficult physical tasks such as cutting logs with a chain-saw. Another respondent, in talking about hockey, argued that PD, a person who had only
played hockey on the frozen ponds around home, could skate circles
around most of the guys from the city. Upon questioning, it turned out that
he was referring to the ability to skate for hours without stopping. An older
man, dressed in a plaid lumberjack-style shirt and a jacket that was open at

the neck in minus twenty Celsius weather, became annoyed at what he thought was the boasting of another local man who had simply remarked, sarcastically, that 'riding snowmobile in this weather was a snap.'

Since, as a number of villagers indicated, poaching frequently required snowmobiling over rough terrain for hours, chasing game on snowshoes up and down hills, dragging quarters of meat for long distances, and being able to survive under severe and dangerous weather conditions, those who are good at it were esteemed for their abilities. Informants labelled such people with the prestigious status of 'outdoorsman' or 'woodsman.'

One aspect which should not be overlooked as a motivation for hunting, both legal and illegal, is the excitement associated with planning and then actually undertaking a hunting trip in the open country on snowmobiles, with a group of like-minded friends (see Mandville, 1974, 5–6 for a description of the feelings of a Newfoundland hunter when a hunting foray is imminent). Wadel writes:

There can be no doubt that the moose meant a lot to George. It not only gave him 'something to do,' but also involved him in much social interaction during the actual hunt. After the hunt, there was much work involved in cleaning, butchering and hanging up the carcass in George's store; and, later, trips to the store to 'cut a slice for dinner' or for a 'snack in the evening.' Also, the hunt was a topic of conversation for the people who came to view the moose. Thus, both the actual hunt and the residual activities increased the range of George's social interaction for some time. (1986, 67)

Felt et al. (1995a, 101) similarly report a seasonal preoccupation of outport residents with the moose hunt.

The level of excitement and adventure is raised when illegal hunting, with its risk of getting caught, is part of the rationale for a winter wilderness ride. In a region where other outlets for recreation and sport are severely lacking, snowmobiling into the uninhabited woods and barrens has become the major winter leisure pursuit. Several people related that their favourite time of the year was February or March, when there was enough snow on the ground to ensure good snowmobiling and the days were getting warmer.

While there was general approval for poaching when the meat was consumed, a number of persons indicated that there were strongly held norms sanctioning the slaughter of animals for non-instrumental reasons. Similar observations have been made by McGrath (n.d. #2) in the Avalon

Peninsula of Newfoundland and Brymer (1990) in the American South. One respondent stated: 'Some of the guys go out there and if there's five moose there, they won't eat the five moose but they'll kill them all. These are the kinds that I would tell on [report on the poacher hot line].' Hunter UA decried the fact that if the slaughter was allowed to go on, 'there would be no moose left for my kids.' Another observer noted that

'not just one but several people in Fish Arm had killed upwards of thirty moose in a year and on a Sunday would go out and knock down a moose on their skidoos just for fun. ... People would go out and find twelve carcasses just left to rot. ... The people themselves were getting sick of that sort of thing.' (Transcribed interview)

Importantly, while there were incidents of the needless slaughter of big game, respondents unanimously said no when asked if there was commercial poaching taking place in the study area.

The Effect of Wildlife Enforcement

The penalties for violations of big game regulations can be quite severe, especially considering the low income and high unemployment in the region. The minimum penalty for violations under the Wildlife Act during the period of field work was a $1000 fine or thirty days in jail for the first offence and a jail sentence of at least thirty days *and* a minimum $3000 fine for a second offence if it occurred within five years of the first. In addition, hunting privileges may be suspended for up to five years, and guns, hunting equipment, boats, vehicles, and practically anything else in the possession of the charged individual capable of being used to kill, store, or transport wild life can be seized and forfeited (Newfoundland and Labrador, 1982).

The severity of these sanctions has thwarted some from poaching. The following notes were recorded in an interview with two fishermen in Main Harbour:

But now, JC said, the fines are pretty stiff. 'If I went after a moose and hauled it back in my truck – Well, my truck is worth $20,000 – that's a pretty expensive moose.' QE said that there is a $3000 to $4000 fine plus you get your snowmobile and rifle confiscated. JC said, 'Who can afford that?' I asked if it was the fines that were a deterrent, and the answer was 'yes.' They noted that now there's ten to twenty times as much moose as there used to be. (Field notes)

Not everyone is deterred, even if they have been jailed for Wild Life violations. Field notes on a convicted poacher by a key informant read:

BI described PN, a guy who was sent to jail over in —— for a month or so for poaching. He said he's fifty-eight or fifty-nine, 'Jesus he's been doing that [poaching] forever. It's just a way of life with him. About a week after he got out of jail, he was right back there hunting again. He'll probably do that until the day he dies. Some people are just moose crazy.'

For those who continue to poach, the possibility of getting caught in the act has forced them to take many precautions. The nature of these precautions varies between the two communities. Fish Arm, the more isolated community, has only two snowmobile routes out into the area where the wildlife is hunted, and the topography of the settlement makes it difficult for snowmobilers to go anywhere unnoticed by other residents. In addition, it is policed by a game warden (YQ), who has the reputation of being a tough outdoorsman and a fearless and dedicated conservationist. Notes from a self-confessed poacher indicate the respect and fear YQ generates:

I asked him about evasive behaviour when the game warden is on your trail, a guy like YQ. He said it's pretty hard to get away once he's on your trail. You might as well give up because there have been cases where people have thrown their guns away and YQ picks them up and brings them back. Or whenever you leave a trail of blood, he'll follow you. (Field notes)

Another respondent said:

YQ has a big advantage because he uses government gas. He can go all winter and it doesn't cost him anything. There is no sense going in the open country if you're trying to get away from him. If you go in the open country, he'll see you and the best thing to do is bury your meat then go to the woods and hope you can lose him. (Field notes, FV)

Strategies for avoiding being caught include hunting during 'dirty' weather (overcast or snowy conditions), hiding rifles in the woods, burying carcasses in the snow, falsely reporting poaching in the hopes that the single game warden will be diverted to a different area, trying to ascertain his location by phone, and so on.

In the Fish Arm area, the interaction between the game warden and some poachers has taken on a game-like flavour, something like the popular portrayal of moonshiner-revenuer relations in the American South. Because the game warden has reputedly waited all night to catch returning poachers along either of the two entrances to the village of Fish Arm and has reportedly even climbed trees to 'ambush' suspicious riders, some poachers have taken to fleeing at sight of him, knowing that a chase will ensue. This is done for excitement on occasions when there is no evidence that could incriminate a person for poaching. The following account illustrates this:

At one point SO was out in the country with two other people just going for a ride. They didn't have any guns on them or anything like that. They saw YG and decided, just for the hell of it, because they didn't have any guns or booze, to take off, knowing YQ would start chasing them. YQ chased them for two hours. They were finally stopped when they came to a sheer cliff. They couldn't go anywhere, so YQ came up to them and searched their skidoos, looking for guns, looking for pieces of moose hair, or anything like that. SO said, 'You wouldn't have caught me if we'd hadn't run into this cliff.' YQ replied, 'Yes, I would have caught you because you guys don't carry any spare gas. I've got two extra containers here. I'd chase you for two days. If it took me two days, I'd get you. (Field notes)

There was a lot of guessing about whether YQ was in the vicinity and what he would do if he were. One observer remarked, 'Some people think they're smarter than YQ,' implying that they most certainly were not. This same respondent also related that people did everything to YQ. 'Cabins he had in the country were wrecked, and someone had even shit on his cabin door' (field notes).

Respondents in the Main Harbour area indicated that poaching goes on, especially during 'dirty days.' The wardens had to come in from a larger town about an hour and a half's drive away, and they were not likely to come in on those (dirty) days (field notes from WM). The amount of poaching seems to be much less than in Fish Arm, perhaps owing to the smaller number of moose locally available and the larger relative population. Large-scale slaughters were much less frequent.

The Impact of Social Relations in the Community

The image that may have been portrayed above of an idyllic village culture that unanimously supports poaching for local consumption is only partly true. Among hunters in the communities studied, competitiveness and tension are generated by the struggle for prestige and by more mundane desires for a full freezer. For example, knowledge of terrain and the location of the moose is esoteric information and closely guarded.[7] Places are often referred to using local names, so that people 'belonging to' Fish Arm and Main Harbour have immense difficulty giving each other directions, and even people from the same outport frequently must give detailed descriptions of sites and locations to convey the exact whereabouts. Attempts have been made to sabotage others' efforts to learn different routes through the unmarked terrain. Several individuals related (in terms which suggested that it was not remarkable) an incident where the ribbons left behind by one group of snowmobilers to mark a new trail were changed around by a second group, a situation which almost resulted in the first group being stranded overnight under severe weather conditions.

Special efforts are made to keep the location of moose sightings from others. 'Did you see any wildlife?' is a common question asked of persons who have been out snowmobiling, even if they are not well known to the person making the inquiry. One is morally obligated to respond to requests for this sort of information from fellow villagers, but frequently attempts are made to conceal specific information from all but a trusted few, especially if one wants the animal for oneself. One well-known hunter said that he sometimes replied 'thousands' when asked if he had spotted any moose on a trip in the country, hoping that this use of exaggeration would make the listener think that he had spotted none. A woman recounted her efforts to keep her eight-year-old child from blurting out the location where they had seen a moose. The effort was to no avail, however, as a person who knew that the child had been in the country on a snowmobile teased the information from her and reportedly went out and shot the moose himself, much to the consternation of the mother. With less ingenious adults, however, the questioner is left to interpret the responses given, based on the verbal and nonverbal cues and the known personality of the respondent.

The recent institution of the toll-free poacher hot line has exacerbated tensions within the community that are normally glossed over by an outward mode of interaction sanctioning verbal aggression. One example of the impact that an anonymous tip has on the party or parties who are reported has already been given, in chapter 4. Likewise, another person who was convicted of poaching through the poacher hot line said, when he was caught, 'It was probably somebody who he thought was a friend, but they didn't turn out to be a friend after all.'

As well as feuding parties, suspicion often centres around strangers, including the professionals in the community who are from the outside and thus less bound and affected by moral and social sanctions in the community concerning aggression. Thus, one informant, who was suspicious of the fact that he had returned with several others from a successful poaching trip on a Monday and the game wardens came Tuesday, felt sure that the local medical professional or someone close to this person had made the phone call.

For those involved in poaching, precautions have to be taken to prevent the possibility of being anonymously reported by others: people with whom a private feud is being waged, jealous hunting rivals, individuals or families who have no access to poached game, or anyone else who might be vindictive. Such people pose an increasing problem for poachers because it is difficult to apply the community social sanctions against villagers without convincing proof of who phoned in the call. It has probably always been difficult to hide hunting activity from others in small isolated settlements where houses are huddled together near the sea, where adults and children work close to home and visit freely, and where few doors are locked: in short, where there is little effective privacy. The potential poacher must be concerned not only with hiding a large carcass but also with the myriad of activities associated with its preservation (cutting and washing the meat, wrapping it for freezing or, if bottling is chosen, purchasing and washing of bottles, a marathon session of boiling the meat, concealing the preserved bottles, and so on). The preservation of the game needs to be done quickly and usually involves the male and female adults living in the household. Given the effective communication networks in small isolated villages like Main Harbour and Fish Arm, concealment from nosy and possibly vindictive neighbours is a difficult task. One advantage, however, is suggested by RX, who stated that 'everyone in Main Harbour knew who was doing most of the moose hunting, and also who were the gossipers and when they went to bed.' Again, because poachers and potential informers typically know each other's patterns of behaviour in depth, poaching behaviour takes on a game-like character, with each group trying to outsmart the other.

Conclusion

In this chapter, I argue that the general patterns of outport poaching described are the result of law enforcement practices, cultural attitudes towards hunting, and consideration of the village context in which poachers must operate. In chapter 6, one particular hunting trip is described in detail, illustrating in more concrete form the way in which the complex considerations suggested in this chapter result in the patterned behaviour.

6

The Modus Operandi of the Poacher: A Case Study

The hunting of big game like moose and caribou in the unforgiving environment of uninhabited, snow-covered woods during winter is a collective activity requiring considerable skill, knowledge, effort, and team work. *Illegal* hunting of such game requires not only the same basic skills as legal hunting, but also a whole set of skills and orientations associated with the precautions and secrecy needed to avoid detection. The following case study describes the circumstances and activity involved on a particular hunting trip.

Research Background

This trip occurred in the winter. By this time I had become a familiar person in Main Harbour, having visited the area previously and, during the more prolonged stay over winter, engaging in social activities like playing darts, playing for a village hockey team, and riding the snowmobile that I had purchased in the knowledge that snowmobiles are more important for local winter travel (and interaction with others) than automobiles. Operating a snowmobile opened the possibility of participation in winter outdoor activities, which are traditionally carried out by men. As I rode around the local area, I often stopped to talk. Most men, being seasonally unemployed in the winter, spent a considerable part of their time outdoors, cutting trees for fuel wood, ice fishing, sealing, and so on. The friendly orientation of most outport residents, the fact that many in the winter had no formal work schedule and often looked forward to a chance to 'have a yarn,' and mutually interesting topics of conversation such as snowmobiles and the outdoors eventually led to my being invited to join in with individuals and small groups as they cut trees or went on short pleasure trips on snowmobiles.

I spent considerable time with one small group of men who were enthusiastic about and competent at many economically oriented traditional outport activities such as setting up snares for rabbits ('tailing slips'), ice fishing on small lakes, cutting fuel wood, and especially moose hunting. Initially, I simply tagged along when they were involved in such activities, doing things like helping to stack logs as they were being cut with a chain-saw. Subsequently I was invited to come along on several snowmobile trips which took an entire day to complete and which included excursions of several hours into wilderness areas. These trips required planning and preparation on the part of those involved. Most of this took place at informal social gatherings at participants' homes. Sometimes topographical maps were brought out and the route discussed, usually over drinks. For those involved, it was clear that such trips were one of the highlights of winter. Though these were not hunting trips, one of the primary preoccupations of the participants was with the type and quantity of wildlife that might be seen (cf. chapter 1). Indeed, sometimes routes were planned so as to check out reports of moose sightings from friends and relatives, or locations thought to be rife with wildlife. This preoccupation with animals did not seem to be peculiar to this particular group; practically all males whom we encountered for several days after such a trip would inquire whether we had seen any wildlife when they learned that we had taken a long trip into the country.[1]

The following account describes events which took place after I had become a more or less regular presence among this small group. (Names and places have been changed to shield the identities of the participants.) This description is based on the detailed account given to me by the participants, particularly Sam, shortly after the hunting trip occurred. The leader of the expedition was Clark, an experienced outdoorsman and avid hunter with a commanding knowledge of the local area. Bert was a local member of the group who was less experienced at hunting and Sam was relatively new to hunting. This account has been italicized to separate it from the rest of the chapter.

The Hunt

Sam received a phone call about 10:30 p.m. from Clark asking if he was busy the next day. When Sam said no, Clark asked if he wanted to go for a snowmobile ride in the country. He said yes. Another member of the group, Bert, was also going along. The time of departure was set for early in the morning, around 8:00 a.m., when the gas station opened. Clark and Bert would call on Sam by skidoo and everyone would set out from Sam's place.

Sam spent the next few hours getting ready clothing, snowmobile, and equipment. This included a large lunch, some liquor and soft drinks, extra clothing, snowshoes, a five-gallon gas container, and mechanical tools. Importantly, it was not mentioned to Sam over the phone that hunting would take place, and this was not made clear until later. The destination was an area known to all three, an area quite remote but accessible by a fairly good snowmobile trail which initially went along an unploughed road. The three men had previously agreed that it would be nice to take such a day-long snowmobile trip, so this trip in the country was not a complete surprise.

The next morning at about 7:30 a.m., Clark phoned Sam and said he and Bert were on the way. Sam had already had breakfast, and it was still before dawn when Clark and Bert arrived by skidoo, Clark towing a covered 'slide' (sled). The slide was a handmade wooden box about five feet in length, to which was attached a pair of skis set apart the same width as the runners on a snowmobile. There were plastic strips attached to the bottoms of the skis to reduce friction. Slides have become increasingly popular in this region, in part, one presumes, because they hide the contents being towed. Some reapportioning of the equipment took place, since Bert had arranged to pick up another slide from an acquaintance, and the three set off to gas up. With that accomplished, they picked up the other slide (also a covered one) and about 8:30 a.m. passed the last house in the outport and the trip began.

The next hour or so was spent riding further into the barren area, first along a wide roadbed and later along a narrower beaten track. The temperature was about minus ten Celsius with a gusting headwind, so the major preoccupation was with the cold. At one point, when the group stopped to admire a sea view from the top of a cliff, Sam mentioned that a draught of cold air was leaking down the arm of his snowmobile suit. Clark solved this problem by tying the sleeve tight with some nylon rope.

As they entered higher elevations, the vegetation changed so that now the trees became shorter and stunted, and in some areas, there was only the scattered bush. The hills were more rounded than the cliffs dotting the ride in. The wind was stronger in the barren area, so strong that in one or two stretches, the snow had blown off the trail. No other persons or vehicles were seen for the duration of the day. The riders drove sitting down and at times crouched behind the snowmobile windshields during this part of the trip, as this seemed more comfortable. Clark, who knew the way best, led, followed by Bert, and Sam brought up the rear. Sometimes Clark, Bert, and Sam drew abreast of each other for a shouted conversation over the din of the snowmobile engines. (It was interesting to note that when groups of outport residents go for a ride in the country, they line up in a straight line whenever they stop, possibly denoting the equity of peers.)

Finally, Clark pulled off the trail at an area known to him from conversation with a relative to be the location of a herd of caribou that was said to be about twenty-five in number. At this point, it became clear to Sam that this trip was actually a hunting trip. (Clark was well known locally as a poacher, and said later that the reason for saying it was just a ride in the country was to avoid overt telephone conversation about illegal hunting.)

Pulling up, Clark took his rifle out of the slide where it was stored and proceeded to load bullets into it. The rifle was carried openly during the rest of the period of hunting. Bert mentioned that this was the first time he had ever hunted illegally, so it was clear that Clark, with his greater woods experience, was the leader. There was a short discussion of the best place to look for moose and caribou. The weather was overcast with some blowing snow, though one could see a few kilometres across the open areas. Clark remarked that the weather was perfect, it being a 'dirty' day with blowing snow, and it was barely possible to tell the direction from the sun. Still, there was enough visibility to see game within shooting range. Clark also commented that there was no need to worry about planes (game wardens or Mounties surveying by air) in such weather. The only concern was the possibility of encountering a game warden on patrol by snowmobile. He jokingly stated that the only worry was about YQ, a warden well known for his zeal in chasing poachers. Clark also pointed out that this area was not YQ's territory to patrol.

The place where they had stopped was on a frozen lake where the water below was flowing quite fast. Clark checked the depth of the ice (and thus its load-bearing capability) by chopping through it with an axe. He was satisfied that it was thick enough here to easily support the weight of snowmobiles. From here on, most of the travelling was over a series of frozen lakes and ponds which made for easy skidoo riding, with occasional forays among the barren hills (the barrens). The mode of riding changed too. Instead of sitting behind the windshields, the riders now knelt up on the seats with one or both legs, looking over the windshield to get a better view of the lake and the shoreline. Heads and helmets turned constantly in the search for large game. The pace of riding slowed as well.

After perhaps an hour of searching for game, the hunting party stopped for some tea. This meant finding a sheltered area with a supply of trees for firewood. They had just started to 'boil up' when Clark noticed a moose which had come out onto the pond they had stopped beside and had turned to look at the snowmobile party. The animal did not appear to be in a particular hurry. Clark later said that it would have run had it caught scent of humans. Jumping on his snowmobile to get closer, Clark took off in the direction of the animal and, pulling up, fired several shots. He appeared to miss and the animal ran back into the woods. (Clark later remarked that there must be something wrong with the rifle, as its sights must be off to miss at that range. Apparently a friend had borrowed it recently and perhaps had done some damage to the gun.) Following by snowmobile, the trio drove into the edge of the woods, where Clark shot the animal again and felled it. In fact, this last bullet went through the moose and came out on the other side, judging from blood spots on the snow where it lay.

At this point Clark and Bert started to field dress the carcass, while Bert suggested that Sam cover up the animal's tracks and blood spatters by dragging a small tree behind the snowmobile over them. In the pure white winter environment, aerial surveillance would have no difficulty spotting the bright red blood trail, snowmobile tracks, and the like. Clark and Bert worked at quartering the animal, using an axe to remove the head, then the hind area, and finally chopping down through the breastbone. Clark was showing Bert how to butcher the animal. A sharp knife was used to cut through the sinew, muscle, and fat after the breast bone was severed. Clark had brought along a file to make sure his knife was sharp enough. With the animal thus opened up, they pulled all the guts out as they would clean a fish and buried all the unwanted refuse in the deep snow. Only the heart was saved. Bert offered Sam a drink of blood still warm from the heart, saying hunters usually drank some, but Sam declined. Continuing with the butchering, they split the backbone lengthwise with an axe, and removed the extremities of the limbs, until all that remained was the carcass. Using hunting knives, Clark and Bert efficiently quartered the animal (leaving three ribs on the back quarter), employing the axe where necessary, and always trying to avoid blood spattering. Sam spent most of the time burying discarded animal parts in the snow. This was quite easy because there were several feet of snow on the ground. All worked with their rackets on. They removed skin by pulling on it and using the knife like a razor to peel it away from the carcass. Within half an hour, all that remained were four quarters of meat, just like those one would see hanging in a butcher shop.[2] There was very little seeping blood.

During the quartering, the men were careful not to get moose hairs on themselves, presumably to avoid detection (rumour had it that game wardens could arrest on the basis of a single hair of poached game, and hairs do not decompose quickly). They decided to bury the quarters as well, as there was still plenty of time left in the day to ride around, and they could be picked up later. All three spent a considerable amount of time removing blood spatters from clothing. As some blood had frozen onto the boots, they had to use the axe or a knife to scrape it away. Clark said that when the fire was lit for lunch, the heat of the fire would melt the blood and it would wash off, so a perfect job was not necessary at this time. Both Clark and Bert wore dark blue or black, quite dirty snowmobile outfits which hid the blood stains better than the lighter clothing that Sam was wearing. Bert said it was a good idea to wear darker clothes for hunting.

Leaving the spot, the three rode further, looking for glimpses of other wildlife. Within half an hour, three caribou were spotted on the open ice of a small lake, and the three men chased them on their snowmobiles. Clark later said that caribou, unlike moose, head for the open areas to get away from danger. The caribou kept together for a few minutes, running at speeds of fifty to fifty-five kilometres per hour. Using the snowmobiles, Clark and Sam isolated one from the other two, much as one sees at the rodeo, and attempted to keep it on the ice-covered lake where the going was easier. At one point they came close to bowling the animal over by almost running into its legs. The animal, however, was quite agile on the ice at speed, and finally ran up a sloping terrain and was let go. Presumably it would have been possible to chase it in the 'harder going' off the lake, but during the conversation right after the chase, Clark said that animals that were 'drove' like that were not good to eat.

After the chase, they decided to stop for lunch, so they sought a location that would offer some firewood and protection from the wind. This was no easy task in the windblown barren area. When they located a spot, they then had to find water, as there was more than a foot and a half of ice on the lake. They found it at an area where the body of water narrowed down and there was a swifter flow beneath the ice, making it thinner and easier to chop through. They filled the kettle, which was simply a galvanized fruit juice can, and took it back to the lunch site, started a fire and cut down a log to sit on. They opened their lunch bags and began to eat their meal. With their greater winter outdoor experience, both Clark and Bert had brought bologna, which they sliced and heated up over the open fire, using branches from trees to cook the meat and toast the bread. The hot sandwiches smelled and tasted great. Sam had brought pork sandwiches which were now frozen, difficult to heat up and less appetizing. Clark and Bert sat on their gloves to prevent their pants from getting damp. At one point Clark said that 'this is what it's all about. Americans come up here and pay big money to do this sort of thing.' Conversation drifted to the speed of the caribou, previous hunting trips, and so on. At about 12:30 lunch was over and the men decided to go for a ride further 'inside' (away from home) before heading back.

During the afternoon, the weather became worse. The increasing snow, however, was seen as a benefit, as it would cover any trace of the hunting activity, including the snowmobile tracks. This was important, as the only reason for going out on a 'dirty' day to the barrens with covered slides would be clear to any local person. When they decided to start back home, they relocated the buried quarters, dug them out and loaded them into one of the slides into which a plastic tarpaulin had been placed (to catch most of the blood, which would seep into the wood of the slide). The trio then refuelled, using gas from five-gallon containers strapped to the snowmobiles, topped up the snowmobile oil, and set off on the return journey. The worsening weather made determining directions difficult, but eventually they relocated the main trail and discussed plans on how to dispose of the meat. One suggestion was to dump the meat close to the outport, but before arriving at a travelled highroad, and Clark and Bert could pick it up in a car, using their wives as a cover for the trip. Clark said that they never bothered with that in the past, they just drove skidoos and slides right up to the house and put the slide in the shed.

The rest of the journey back was uneventful, with no stops or conversation, as it was by now getting dark. No other snowmobiles or persons were spotted. Shortly before getting back to the village, the group stopped and, turning off the machines, finalized plans to return without raising suspicion. They decided to use a twisty trail through the woods behind most of the houses to avoid being seen with the covered slides. This plan was the one that they adhered to. As the house Sam was staying at was the closest one, he left Clark and Bert there, and they reached their own homes without any problems. (Adapted from field notes)

The Preparation and Distribution of the Meat

The preceding account describes the actual hunting, field quartering, and transporting back to the village of a moose shot illegally. The work of the poacher does not stop here, however. The division of the quarters of

meat and preparation and preservation of the meat must be done quickly, and usually requires the co-operation and services of members of one's
kin network. The following section of the chapter provides details of this
aspect of the hunting trip described above.

*After a full day of hunting and snowmobiling in the country, Sam took a short nap.
Wakening, he phoned Clark, to whose home the quarters had been taken, to find out what
further tasks needed to be done. Heeding warnings from friends about not directly mention-
ing the animals or activity on the phone (the phones being presumed to have party lines or
someone who could listen in, though they are now all private lines), Sam then drove by
automobile to Clark's place. Clark said that Bert had company that night, and would be
unable to help out (which was expected of all participants) until much later, after the
company left. Indeed, it was considered a good idea not to begin until after Clark's children
had gone to sleep, since children were likely to blurt out anything. In addition, starting out
late at night made it unlikely that anyone would just drop in and see what was going on.
The other advantage of disposing of the meat late in the evening was that it lessened the
likelihood of neighbours becoming suspicious about activities, and possibly reporting. This
fear was heightened by the fact that a local person had recently been reported, probably on
the SPORT or anonymous poaching hot line, and had been found by the game wardens in
possession of illegal meat.*

*Sam arrived at Clark's home at approximately 11:00 p.m. The moose quarters were
hanging in the woodshed, which had electricity and lights but no running water. Clark and
Sam obtained water in large pails from a small stream nearby, then set to work cutting up
the moose quarters, washing the pieces and bagging them in freezer bags. The water was cold
and the shed unheated, and it quickly became clear that washing the relatively clean meat
was a waste of time. Thereafter, Clark cut up the moose into chunks using a sharp knife
and occasionally an axe, and Sam packed them away unwashed. This, however, was an
aberration from existing practices. Prior to this, Clark and Sam had taken the precaution
of covering over the window of the shed with close-fitting cardboard to block out light
shining outside, so as to avoid suspicion from passers-by and neighbours. Clark's comment
on the family next door was that they were not that nosy and would not report anything
anyway. However, caution overruled, and with the door closed and the window covered, it
was possible from the outside only to see some small cracks of light coming from the shed.
The weather was very windy and snowy, almost white-out conditions, which helped matters,
since few people would be outside at that hour of the night and even if they were, they might
not notice the bit of light coming from the shed. The chopping noise from the axe was also
muffled somewhat by the blowing wind. Clark, however, did not seem overly concerned about
the amount of noise.*

*Conversation during this time concentrated mostly on the carving of the meat. Comments
like 'Here's a nice roast' and 'This is a twenty-dollar rack of ribs at ——— ' (name of a local*

food store) were common. At one point, they had to decide what to do with all the game. The ultimate decision was Clark's, as he was the one who did the shooting. A portion of meat would be given to the relative who had assisted by giving information on the location of the caribou herd, in spite of the fact that a moose was felled, not a caribou. Each hunter (i.e., each person who went on the hunt) would get an equal share of the remainder. Clark stated, 'That's the trouble with three [hunters]. It's always hard to split up the meat.' When the cutting up was finished, they washed the shed over with warm water and Javex to get rid of some of the blood stains and cleaned the tools and rope. After this was done, the shed looked too clean. Clark said that some dirt ought to be spread around the place, which he did. The snow outside the shed was inspected and a few small blood spots covered by kicking at the snow. Clark said he would use a shovel later to finish the job. Sam placed his portion of the meat in boxes and took them home.

While they were at Clark's house, he received a phone call from the relative who had provided the original information about the location of the caribou herd. Asked if he got anything, Clark replied that they had had some luck. Again, the concern with avoiding overt references on the phone was evident, as was the pride of the successful hunter.

The next morning, Clark received a phone call from another friend who requested that a borrowed item be returned. As this person was familiar with poaching himself, the fact that Clark's kitchen was now stacked up with bottles and large pots for boiling meat in preparation for bottling the moose was seen as problematic. Clark said he would return the item himself. He later related that even if the friend dropped over, he would keep him in the basement where he would not be able to see the bottling preparations.

Another problem was the supply of caps for the preserving bottles. To bottle the meat safely, new caps were needed. Clark's solution to this was to buy some from a store that was not the nearest one he would normally go to. As he anticipated some questioning from the store clerk (partly in view of his reputation as a poacher), he prepared an answer in advance. He would say that he was going to bottle up some seal which he had caught. He even had a bottle of seal at home which could be used as evidence that this was what he was up to.

Later that evening, Sam returned to Clark's home to find that Clark's wife had bottled up most of their portion of the meat, and the kitchen was hot and humid. She marked the bottles that were done with a date that would indicate that they were bottled in the fall, when the moose licence that Clark had in his possession was valid. Meanwhile, Clark had boiled some water and placed the empty slide in the basement close to the stove where it had started to thaw out. Using a scraper, Sam and Clark removed blood-soaked snow and ice and all the animal hairs they could find. Finally, the entire inside of the slide was wiped with warm water until no trace of blood was left.

The aim of this chapter has been to give a detailed account of one particular episode of big game hunting. Other snowmobile trips (not necessarily for hunting purposes, but in which the spotting of big game was always a central preoccupation) and numerous conversations with other hunters in the two Newfoundland outports studied lead me to believe that the concerns and behaviour described on this trip are not atypical.

7

Moonshine

Just as hunting has its roots in the traditional outport economy and has become part of a cultural tradition, so has the home manufacture and consumption of alcohol. The manufacture of alcoholic beverages undoubtedly has been affected by the geographical isolation and relative poverty of inhabitants of outport communities. Historically, bottled liquor was purchased in the outports from sailing vessels that occasionally plied the Newfoundland waters. However, the lack of cash income in the outports combined with the tradition of self-sufficiency in domestic production spurred on the home manufacturing of alcoholic beverages. The beverages produced included homebrew (made from malt and yeast and occasionally some fruits), spruce beer (made from spruce boughs and molasses) and a variety of other homemade drinks such as wines, brandy, gins and so on, and moonshine (cf. Andrews and Wells, 1973).

Moonshine differs from other alcoholic beverages that have been made in Newfoundland in that it requires the use of a distilling process. While it is perfectly legal to make other alcoholic beverages, with Confederation it became illegal in Newfoundland to make moonshine. This unique illegal status and the ambiguous outport community sentiments surrounding moonshine (described below) have resulted in a custom of secrecy shrouding this activity. It is difficult for strangers, even native Newfoundlanders who are acquainted with people in the community, to break through the reluctance of those involved in the activity (e.g., Andrews and Wells). Thus, in spite of the fact that many studies of the Newfoundland outports indicate the prevalence among men of drinking alcohol on major social occasions, in regard to the moonshine, there is an almost total lack of written accounts. The major sources of written information on moonshine that I located were student interviews of relatives who were involved in this activity collected by the Memorial University of New-foundland's Folklore and Language Archive (Quigley, 1981; Brazil, 1979; Andrews and Wells, 1973) and other local sources. These are referred to in the relevant sections below.

Moonshine as an Ignored Social Problem

As a result of his own examination of research papers in Memorial University's Folklore Archives, Quigley (1981, 16–19) constructed a map indicating that references to moonshine could be found across the island of Newfoundland. Several outports on the northeast coast, the location of the present study, were mentioned. Despite this prevalence, however, moonshining has received little notice from the mass media or government officials, including the police. Field notes of an interview with a police officer whose jurisdiction included Main Harbour reveal local police attitudes:

Now, I asked at one point about the problem of moonshine. Constable B said that he didn't know there was any moonshine out there but that he would have to keep his eyes open for it (now that I had drawn his attention to it). Moonshine, then, is something which not all the police are aware of as existing, much less a problem out in this area. 'What's done is done very privately,' said the other constable, who was in listening range of the interview. 'You know, not for public consumption.'

Similarly, field notes from an interview about moonshine with the judge who covered Main Harbour read: 'He seemed to sort of shrug it off with a little bit of a smile. I don't think that in the judge's view, moonshine was any sort of a problem at all.'

The fact that, in the outports studied, moonshine was made and consumed privately has contributed to the lack of public attention given the matter. This could be compared to the situation when alcoholic beverages are distilled for commercial profit, as in parts of the American South, notably Kentucky, or in Newfoundland's south coast, where 'rum-running' or the illegal importation of liquor from the French islands of St Pierre and Miquelon has recently become a newsworthy social issue (Walsh, 1991). Commercial distillation of liquor, of course, results in loss of public revenue and may be expected to be pursued more vigorously than acts of private manufacture for consumption by oneself and perhaps a few others.

Another reason for the lack of police and public attention on outport moonshining is the general decline of the practice over the past several decades. The increasing availability of store-bought liquor and the spread of licensed drinking establishments, combined with the increasing ability to afford mass-produced products as the outports emerged from the cashless mercantile system, have resulted in moonshine becoming less popular (cf. Quigley, 1981, 18–19; Andrews and Wells, 1973, 9).

An interview with one of Main Harbour's oldest citizens reveals the general level of past consumption of moonshine. This respondent said that there was 'an awful amount of moonshine in —— (a neighbouring logging community) when he worked there. He remembered the time when Charles Smallwood, Joey Smallwood's father, was working with the lumber company and was sent out to get some moonshine because there wasn't enough money for liquor' (field notes, GG). Likewise, a younger fisherman recalled that in his father's day, liquor bought from schooners was only used on special occasions such as Christmas, where a small amount was offered to each person present. He demonstrated the ritual involved in pouring out the precious fluid and the simultaneous lifting of the glasses. The rest of the time, moonshine was drunk. These accounts are corroborated by the description, by a woman from a nearby community who was born in 1891, of Christmas socials in which everyone went from house to house 'and, of course there would always be a bottle of moonshine to drink' (Hewitt, 1978, 37).

Comparing life in the community between the 1960s and 1970s, a resident of a northeast coast outport notes the decline in the production of home-manufactured alcoholic beverages:

Ten years later, there was very little dogberry wine and the moonshine can had to be stowed away in the cellar from brass buttons ... With the introduction of breweries and controllers,[1] home made beer was no longer needed for the old type refreshment ... Most people on Christmas now, can be seen with a case of beer, a bottle of whiskey or their favorite bottle of rum. Instead of the home made wine, the champagne and Cold Duck wine has taken over the Christmas dinner table. (Brown, 1975, 57–8)

Field Work

The empirical data in this chapter are a direct result of my long period of contact with a number of outport citizens in both Main Harbour and Fish Arm, some of whom made, as well as consumed, moonshine. Indeed, much of what is related in this chapter is the result of information I received from individuals who were initially quite silent about their involvement with moonshine, but who, after shared experiences of snowmobiling together, or playing hockey or darts and sharing beer or liquor, eventually were much more apt to reveal information, or offer me a drop of moonshine at appropriate times. Reciprocal offers of a beer or a drink certainly helped establish convivial social relationships. Snowmobile trips, parties at cabins, and other activities by small groups were especially likely to involve the consumption of illegally manufactured alcohol. The interest I expressed in moonshine resulted in gifts of bottles of the liquid from a few individuals, indicating that they trusted me enough to assume that at the very least they would not get into trouble by revealing their own involvement to an outsider.

Community Norms regarding Alcohol Consumption during Public Celebrations

In order to understand patterns of moonshine consumption and production, it is helpful to understand general patterns of drinking in the outports. Most written work by academics emanates from the golden age of outport research in the 1960s and 1970s and focuses on alcohol consumption during 'times' or 'occasions' or at public forums where its use is normative and ritualized. Szwed lists some of these occasions in a Codroy Valley village on the west coast of Newfoundland in the mid-1960s:

drinking has become a necessity for all public gatherings: now weddings, funerals, Christmas, New Year's, Easter, dances, political meetings, the meetings of the board, and all *ad hoc* meetings have become the occasion of heavy drinking. (1966, 106)

During these public celebrations, alcohol consumption takes on specific cultural patterns. The passage from Faris' study of Cat Harbour on the northeast coast briefly describes some of the drinking norms at weddings:

Drinking can become heavy at weddings, for as soon as the parental supply is exhausted, the groom is obligated to supply and many individuals will have brought their own. As the consumption is exclusively by males and in the confines of the parental home, the order of entertainment is sexual joking and risqué 'cuffers.' (1973, 159)

I observed weddings at both Main Harbour and Fish Arm. After the wedding ceremony in the church, a meal is served, requiring, in some cases, two sittings to accommodate everyone. After the meal, the dishes are cleared and the hall or lodge is prepared for the dance. The men tend to disperse into homes and meeting places, drinking with a few friends, making an appearance at the dance only much later, often inebriated. The dance itself is a lively and extended affair, with people of all ages talking, dancing, and drinking together from a never-ending supply of beer and liquor. Sometimes a band is hired, but more often a disk jockey who can play a variety of tunes, both rock and roll and Newfoundland music. In Fish Arm, on occasion, a local fiddle player is requested to play a jig, particularly one to which some of the local people can perform a long and complicated local dance. The festivities carry on well into the night and often into the next morning, with many participants becoming visibly inebriated. At one Fish Arm wedding, the groom, dressed in a rented tuxedo, danced until dawn, at which point, still dressed in formal attire, including pants which were by then worn through at the cuff from dancing, he went fishing. Others continued the celebration. Young teenagers can be observed trying to obtain drinks, and are often successful.

Another community-approved occasion for heavy drinking in public is Christmas. Outport Newfoundlanders celebrate the twelve days of Christmas, beginning on Christmas Day and ending on Old Christmas, 6 January. Work essentially stops during this period. It is a time for visiting and for 'times.' One Fish Arm resident recounted the story of how one Christmas he and some other young male friends planned to call on each house through the village, drinking their hosts dry as they worked their way down the road. At the first house, the host, upon hearing of their plan, said, 'Well, you'll have some drinking to do then,' and produced a full case of liquor, saying 'There's plenty more when you finish this.' The young men never got past Uncle ——'s house that night.

Detailed descriptions of the peculiar cultural practice of 'mummering' or 'janneying' that occurs in outport Newfoundland are provided by Sider (1986) and Chiaramonte (1979). Mummering, though a declining practice, still takes place in both Main Harbour and Fish Arm and is another socially approved time for heavy drinking and general revelling. On two separate occasions, I observed at first hand the current practice of mummering. The practice involves a divergence from usual outport behaviour: mummers, who invariably are familiar to people in the house, knock loudly on the door and ask, in voices disguised by talking while inhaling, 'Mummers allowed in?' The mummers are dressed in bulky costumes and head coverings that conceal their identity, and are often cross-dressed, with men dressed like women and vice versa. A Newfoundland jig is played and the mummers boisterously dance. A drink is offered to each, often moonshine, and a process of guessing the identity of each mummer is engaged in. When the identities are ferreted out, the mummers unmask and often further drinks and food are offered. The mummers then go on to the next target house.

It is noteworthy that, in general, because moonshine is illegal, its consumption is less likely to occur in public forums or at 'times' where there are large numbers of people present. The exception is during mummering, but since this practice occurs only among people who are so familiar with each other that their identities can be established even when extensive attempts are made to conceal them, it might not necessarily be considered an exception.

The Social Context of Small Group Drinking in the Outport

Most drinking of moonshine occurs in small groups, among people who consider each other friends and are often related by kinship or marriage. This section describes the cultural and social contexts which give rise to the unique patterns of small group drinking in the outports. These conditions undoubtedly differ significantly from patterns found elsewhere in North America.

There is generally an early and extensive introduction to drinking of alcohol in the outports. Several factors contribute to this. First, unlike urban areas where age homogeneity among companions is more notable, there is a greater tendency in the outports for individuals to interact with persons of a wider range of ages. This is partly a function of numbers. In a large urban or suburban school, the physical basis of friendship formation is the classroom, where everyone in the same class is about the same age. Each age cohort passes through schooling in lockstep fashion. In the small schools in the outports, there may only be a few people of approximately the same age.[2] Consequently, a wider range of ages is notable in friendship groupings. One young Fish Arm teenager, when asked why she was going out with a male in his early twenties, pointed out that there was no one else who was available in the community. Such friendship patterns increase the likelihood of early introduction to alcohol, as older members of the group can supply alcohol to those who are under age.[3]

Particularistic relationships, or the extensive knowledge of familiar others, also tend to break down segregation on the stark demographic basis of age. This is especially notable at 'times' like weddings where three or four generations of people, both kin and those not related, will drink and dance together. Close interaction between youths and adults during such times undoubtedly results in desires for full adult participation among those who are younger, including drinking. Also, the fact that people are treated as individuals reduces the likelihood that a restriction on drinking solely due to age will be enforced. Finally, the egalitarian ethos of the outport supports similar treatment for youths and adults.

Among those aged approximately thirty and older, adult tasks tended to have been thrust upon them early. One woman, now in her early forties, related that by age nine she had been sent out to babysit for her older sister's children, including changing their diapers, making meals, and cleaning house. Another man only in his thirties recounted that he was fishing as a full 'shareman' on his father's boat at age twelve, a fact that was corroborated by the father. The pattern of early assumption of adult responsibilities corresponds with a generally early introduction to adult social activities, including the consumption of alcoholic beverages as a rite of passage.

All of the above factors, combined with the identification of 'times' with alcohol consumption, contribute to the nearly ubiquitous imbibing of alcohol by outport males and a significant proportion of females. The major exception to the pattern of almost universal enjoyment of at least the occasional alcoholic drink occurs among those who belong to a religious denomination that frowns upon alcohol, such as the Salvation Army or the Pentecostal Church.

The extent and patten of outport drinking in small groups among males have been affected by the lack of full-time employment in the outports. Lack of employment has had two major effects. The more obvious one is the greater amount of time available for the unemployed person to engage in drinking. As indicated in chapter 1, for a substantial and (given the current state of the economy of rural Newfoundland) a growing segment of the population, the pattern of seasonal work has meant an increase in potentially idle time.[4] The amount of idle time, however, has been reduced by the necessity of engaging in domestic production to supplement often low wages and government transfer benefits (including unemployment insurance benefits and, more recently, funds from government programs to deal with the moratorium, referred to as 'the package'; see chapter 10 for more details).

The other major impact of lack of employment is its social psychological effect on drinking. Wadel (1986) has described the effect on an outport person of the attack on self-esteem associated with lack of employment for the able-bodied. A list of known heavy drinkers in Main Harbour and in Fish Arm would undoubtedly include many seasonally employed workers, but in general, it is difficult to attribute drinking patterns to the fact of unemployment per se in the outports because almost all the men, fishermen included, are eligible for and do collect unemployment insurance at some point during the year. If there is a relationship between drinking and employment, it may well be that those who are working full time do not have the same opportunity to go have a 'time' which might very well last well into the night and involve prodigious consumption of alcohol. Woodsmen who work all week away from Main Harbour, for example, must wait until the weekend to engage in significant drinking. Fishermen who tend gill nets in the summer are out from before dawn till after dark. Finally, the relationship between lack of employment and drinking is unclear because there is a variety of other causes of drinking, including family tensions, work tensions, boredom, and so on.

Community Reaction to Heavy Drinkers

Many men drink, occasionally quite heavily, but benefit from a general tendency in the community to avoid public labelling and stigmatizing of individuals unless there are unavoidable social problems associated with their behaviour. At one wedding in Main Harbour, for example, two well-known local drinkers passed out on chairs in the middle of the hall and had to be moved to one side, but were essentially ignored by others ('so-and-so passed out again'). A married man with children who worked operating logging machinery was mentioned by a number of persons in private to be an alcoholic who was always drinking, even on the job, but inasmuch as he continued to work and to participate in local community activities (often with liquor on his breath), he was generally well regarded in most other ways. Several other people known for their appetite for liquor, and about whom stories of weekend 'times' were often circulated, were never referred to as 'alkies' or 'alcoholics' or summarily dismissed as such.

A common pattern is for individuals who have an extraordinary attachment to liquor to be treated more as nuisances than as full-blown deviants, provided the drinking does not cause problems. Thus, one fellow in his twenties habitually dropped in on just about any house in Fish Arm that was entertaining company, and where beer or liquor was likely to be served. Remarks were made about his uncanny ability to smell liquor from miles away. He would just drop in and join in the conversation, expecting, and usually receiving, a drink of whatever alcoholic beverage was being served. It was said that 'you could not insult this person enough to get him to leave.' One respondent mentioned that on one occasion when she had other company, she became annoyed by him and tried to drive him out by slapping him really hard. She said she slapped him so hard that it brought tears to his eyes, but even this did not deter him or alter his demeanor. 'Do it again, if you want' was his reaction. The fact that he was viewed as 'harmless,' and in addition was seen as generous in reciprocally providing liquor when he could, resulted in his being able to continue his behaviour.

A visit by a known heavy drinker is likely to result in an offer of a drink. Thus, a retired fisherman who rarely offered beer to others was prompt to offer one to a neighbour who occasionally dropped by, later acknowledging in private that the drink was what his neighbour really wanted. A younger Main Harbour resident described an incident where he violated the local custom by intentionally refusing to offer a local visitor a beer. He had been outside working and drinking a beer when the visitor, a neighbour, came around. The visitor never directly asked for a beer, but the description of his attempts to have one offered was hilarious. He would watch, almost licking his lips, his eyes glued to the movement of the beer bottle as the resident continued to drink without offering him one. Eventually, the neighbour left without being successful in getting a drink. The resident said that 'people like that would stay until they drank every drop you had, if you let them.' However, the resident's behaviour was classed as 'miserable' by others.

The lenient treatment and hesitation to label and differentially treat those who drink heavily in the outports are certainly part of the general inhibition of aggression that has been noted as a general theme of outport culture (Faris, 1973; Sider, 1986, etc.). Those who are viewed as harmful, by regularly becoming violent, and those whose behaviour cannot easily be excused as being the result of occasional over-indulgence either reduce their drinking or leave the community, voluntarily or involuntarily. Chapter 8 provides an in-depth treatment of interpersonal crime and violence in the outports.

Current Patterns of Outport Drinking

The current pattern of outport drinking has been affected by the cultural responses to economic and social realities of outport life. As mentioned above, the lack of employment leaves many men with time on their hands. Moreover, the lack of recreational facilities and the geographical isolation limit activity. In a culture where (as noted in chapter 1) there is a strong division of labour along gender lines and 'the house is the woman's castle, not the man's' (Wadel, 1986, 57), men spend much of their free time in the woods, cutting logs or doing other chores, or in their 'stores' or wooden sheds, which are typically built apart from the house. These stores in particular have become places where men sit and chat with friends, often over drinks. On a recent visit to Fish Arm, another male visitor and I were walking down the road when we observed five or six local adults ranging in age from about twenty to about forty sitting about in a large store located alongside the road. Knowing a couple of these people, we were invited in for a beer. Shortly afterwards, we were offered a drink of moonshine from a bottle produced by one of the men. Conversation revealed that, with all fishermen and fish plant workers idled by the moratorium on fishing, a number of men who drifted in and out of this popular meeting location whiled away a lot of time talking and drinking.

Current modes of alcohol consumption are also affected by community-supported traditional values of hard work and the social sanctioning of persons seen as 'lazy.' This ensures that most men, mindful of how others in the community view them, take pains to keep busy and to appear busy (cf. Wadel, 1986, ch. 6) or to avoid interaction with others that would indicate idleness. Thus, overt displays of extended drinking during week-days are avoided. Much of the heavy drinking takes place in cabins built in the woods which provide a haven away from the eyes and gossip of the village, where friends and relatives can meet and engage in socially approved of activities such as cutting wood, hunting, and so on.

Some men, especially those who are younger and less affected by community values, regularly pursue activities that have no instrumental economic value, such as going for a snowmobile ride or to someone's cabin primarily to drink and have a 'time.' To the extent that these individuals are seen as engaging in a life style revolving around 'sport' and based on unemployment insurance, they attract the consternation, but also the envy, of others. Thus, one full-time employee of a utility company complained that his life style was not any better than that of people on 'pogey,' and in fact it was worse because he did not have the time to 'sport around' as they did. Field notes from a conversation with a teacher indicate similar sentiments:

RK revealed that he probably made twice as much as a person would on unemployment, but they seemed to be doing just as well as he was. They might be making twelve or thirteen thousand a year. He seemed able to just get by from month to month, but so were the others. They go get their own firewood, rabbits and so on.

The attractiveness of a life style based on seasonal employment, unemployment insurance, and 'sporting around' has not been lost on many young people. Field notes taken from the same interview with two high school teachers support this point:

RK said that what students really want to do is 'be off most of the winter, cut a few sticks, have a few beers and so on.' This problem was made worse by the fact that many of the parents don't read or write, and collect unemployment most of the winter themselves.

XR added: 'Look at us. We're almost despised by the students around there because what looks good to them is going into the woods for a ride with a case of beer with some other people. People around here can make it on unemployment, unlike a lot of other places.'

For many younger adults, the high level of unemployment in rural Newfoundland has created, years before the rest of North America, a generation X who have little prospect of employment and little faith that even higher education will be of benefit.

RK said that of the few that did go to university, in a couple of cases they quit after just a couple of weeks and came back to the bay. The other students, pointing to them, took the attitude that they wouldn't be able to do any better, and would probably do worse. This was seen as a reason or excuse for not really trying.

XR said that most did not really care what marks they got. 'For most students, it doesn't matter whether they get a 20 or 80. It's all the same.'

Field notes from the interview with both teachers indicated that alcohol was a major problem with students. RK said, 'On a Monday morning some of the students won't show up for class and everyone will know what happened. They got drunked up on the weekend.' Moonshine was a fairly extensive problem even at the high school level, with some not only drinking it, but making it as well.

Finally it should be noted that drinking patterns among men have also been strongly affected by the lack of a significant police presence in the outports noted in chapter 2. Because there is a possibility, however small, that a police patrol will happen along in Main Harbour, there is less open public drinking than in Fish Arm. In Fish Arm, with no police presence, it is easy to observe adults and under-age teenagers drinking on the public dock and in a number of other gathering places in full view of those passing by.

Moonshine Drinking and Social Bonds

Almost all of the drinking or even discussion of moonshine was observed in small groups, among those who were known to participate in, or be supportive of, the practice. Offering a drink of moonshine thus reaffirms the social relationships among those who are included. Most of this drinking takes place in private residences or in cabins in the woods. Drinking moonshine also occurs, however, when small groups of men (sometimes accompanied by wives and girlfriends) meet each other in a public place. Usually, this will be away from the prying eyes of the outport, such as on a snowmobile trip or alongside the road, when, say, friends pass each other and decide to stop and chat. On these occasions, if someone has taken along a flask of moonshine, it will likely be shared.

Today, we were at WM's home. He was outside fixing someone's skidoo. While we were there, three local persons, including the owner of the skidoo, came by. When the skidoo repair was completed, we all decided to go for a little ride up to the pond that supplied the village with water, to check the level, and we did. We decided to go back to WM's house by a different route which involved riding over a fairly rough trail. We would drive for five or ten minutes, then stop for a break. Everyone would stop, I noticed, with their machines parked side by side in a straight row, with none ahead of the others. WM had a bottle of 'shine,' so on these stops everyone would have a couple of swigs. It was remembered as a good time. As one of the riders commented later, 'That's where you get a lot of fun, you know, a bunch of guys going out and doing that.'

Accounts of moonshine consumption almost always emphasize the consumption of large quantities in the context of a 'time.' The following field notes report what happened prior to and during a hockey game involving the village team:

Most of the players were in their twenties going into their thirties. There were a couple of teenagers. One of the players actually barfed in the truck on the way to the game. They had to pull over to the side of the road. Apparently he had been out drinking the night before. The bench smelled like a brewery (from a couple of people sweating out the alcohol), but the talk in the dressing room from those who had been there was about what a good time was had and how much liquor was drunk. KP said he had a full vinegar bottle of shine. Someone asked, 'Oh, one of those 110 ounce bottles?' KP said he thought it was 55 ounces. At any rate, it was a lot of moonshine. (Field notes)

Being in the company of a group known to consume moonshine put me in the position where it was assumed that at the very least, no harm would come from revealing moonshine secrets.

After the long snowmobile ride, the three of us stopped at the Club in ——, a community close to Main Harbour. The bartender, a woman of about fifty years, knew one of my companions, and started talking about what happened to her husband and her when they went on a snowmobile ride last weekend out to someone's cabin. She said that eventually twenty or twenty-five people showed up and they had so much moonshine they lit the lanterns with it. She said everybody had the equivalent of two forty-ouncers at least, and she couldn't understand how so much booze could be drunk. (Field notes)

An indication of the use of moonshine to bind social ties was the pattern, noted above, of producing a flask during a stop on a snowmobile trip. Participants sometimes drank from it, each in turn. Store-bought liquor, on the other hand, was never shared from the bottle in the way that moonshine frequently is.

The Method of Moonshine Production

A comparison of descriptions of the basic method of making moonshine in the outports indicates little variation from area to area (Quigley, 1981; Brazil, 1979; Andrews and Wells, 1973). It is not a complicated task. Unlike hunting, it does not require social interaction with others, though the learning of the technique necessitates interaction with a trusted other, and it is likely that the techniques are often passed from father to son (Brazil, 1979). The ingredients and equipment used in Newfoundland were, and are, readily available to even those in the most remote outports: molasses or brown sugar, yeast, water, a large container (usually a five-gallon plastic tub) for fermenting the 'brew' or 'beer,' a 'can' (sometimes just a large juice can) for boiling the mixture, and some tubing to run through cold water to condense the liquid.

Brown's description of the pre-Confederation method of making moonshine in Fish Arm is instructive:

By New Year's Eve most of the refreshment stocks is just about depleted and yeast cake and molasses is again mixed and placed behind the old comfort wood stove to brew. The process of running of the beverage called moon shine begins with about anywhere from six to eight feet of copper tubing. The tube has several round rings and it is bent to the point where it can fit inside the spout of a two or three gallon tin can. The rings on the far end is submerged in a bucket of ice water and the end bent over the edge of the bucket is placed onto a jug. Once the brew has reached a boiling point the steam disintegrated in the cool water and came from the end of the tube as clear as crystal and almost as powerful as dynamite. In order to keep from loosing [sic] steam from the top and spout of the can, dough was made out of flour and water. This dough was placed around the stopper of the can and the spout where the tube was connected, this served as a seal and no steam or shine was lost. (Brown, 1975, 56)

Some improvements on the basic technique were employed by informants. Respondent WM told about an older man who had come from Ontario and was now living in the area. In spite of his age, this individual showed a lot of interest in traditional outport activities including hunting, trapping, and so on. WM and another local person showed him how they made moonshine. The older person, who was quite resourceful, went to —— (a city) and had stainless steel cans made up for running off the moonshine.

Since the can itself is the most important piece of equipment for distilling shine, it is hidden from practically everyone. However, the borrowing of someone's can for the purpose of running shine was mentioned by several people while I was present.

Occasionally, makers of moonshine will experiment with the basic procedure. One well-known Main Harbour tippler said he sometimes added various fruits and berries to the fermenting mixture to achieve a different taste, but generally he made straight, ordinary moonshine. A heavy-drinking logger from Main Harbour described how he used burnt sugar to colour the clear liquid. By adjusting the amount of burnt sugar added, he could make the moonshine look like Captain Morgan light or dark rum, or rye whisky, depending on what store-bought liquor bottle he was using as a flask. He indicated that this was important for avoiding suspicion and possible trouble with the police.

The quality of one's moonshine invariably refers to the strength of the drink; that is, the relative alcohol content. A fisherman boasted that moonshine was '150 proof, easy, because there's no problem to get a blue flame from it.' Store-bought liquor, in contrast, is usually 80 proof, or 40 per cent alcohol by content. Others told stories of using moonshine to light lanterns, and several times individuals who offered a drink of moonshine used a match or lighter to set a spoonful alight, to indicate its potency.

Overall, there was very little concern with altering the taste of the moonshine or attempting to make it more like store-bought liquor. In both Main Harbour and Fish Arm, it is often mixed with Seven-Up, which only slightly changes the flavour and sweetens it. On one occasion shortly after I began observing outport behaviour, I mixed moonshine with Southern Comfort, a sweet Kentucky bourbon, to try to offset what I thought was the raw taste of the moonshine. The result was a mellow but still very strong drink, which all four men present enjoyed. However, I never saw anyone subsequently consume this particular combination, or mix moonshine with other liquors. For consumers of moonshine, many of whom drink heavily, variations in the taste of the moonshine probably mean little compared to the alcoholic content. In addition, there is a sense of cultural continuity through producing moonshine in the traditional way. Local pride in moonshine seems to revolve around the care taken to produce a good quality traditional product. One person described the stringent procedures he used to prepare the beer and to run it off, producing just one gallon of moonshine and then throwing all of the remaining mixture out. It was more wasteful, but he compared his product favourably to what others produced, particularly those who run off more than a gallon, or who use impure pond water. He explained that the bottle of moonshine that I received from another acquaintance which had turned green had done so because of algae or other impurities in the water.

The Social Distribution of Moonshine Production

Inasmuch as there are likely to be more people who drink moonshine than make it, this section deals with who is likely to be engaged in making it. This was fairly difficult to answer definitively. It is easy to infer the involvement of some individuals because they openly indicate possession of it. In one case, for example, a local resident met up with more than a dozen people while snowmobiling and took the opportunity to offer a drink to anyone who wanted one, from a flask he carried. Because this person had done this on other occasions, it was taken for granted that he was making his own. Telling stories of adventures that involve drinking moonshine with any regularity will also indicate that a person is either making it himself or has close access to someone who is making it. On the other hand, one individual who was well known to me for several years only recently indicated his participation in the manufacture of moonshine by, without any request and comment, leaving me with a bottle of his own product. I was surprised to find out that this person, who subsequently was found to be quite knowledgeable in the production of moonshine, was involved in moonshining at all, for there had been no indication from previous conversations that this was the case.

The manufacture of moonshine is predominantly one that is carried out by mature adult males. Of those personally known to be involved, the youngest was about thirty years old. Most were married with children.[5] Younger people are likely to be less involved in the manufacture of moonshine because of the increased availability of store-bought liquor and beer, the likelihood of living with parents and thus not having as easy access to room for preparing the alcohol, and generally less interest in traditional activities anyway.[6] For the younger generation exposed to television and video rentals, there is a noticeable lessening of interest in cultural artifacts of the traditional way of life in general. Women sometimes drink moonshine, but there was no indication over the research period that any woman had actually engaged in making it by herself.

Making one's own moonshine is almost a necessity for those who drink a lot and cannot easily afford to buy liquor in the store or at a Club or tavern.[7] Drinking a lot is, of course, relative, a point to keep in mind, given the substantial consumption of alcohol during many of the occasions or 'times' that mark the outport calendar of social events. Sometimes, even the home production of liquor is not enough. For example, one person well known in Main Harbour for his drinking habits mentioned, over a beer at the Club, that he was going to make a trip to St John's. His concern was in getting a bottle of 'shine' to take with him.

I said, 'Well, don't you make your own?' He said, 'Yes, I had planned to take two bottles, but I drank them. Then I loaned my car to a friend and he said he would give me a bottle and that's what I'm going to take with me.' (Field notes, KP)

There is some connection between economic circumstances and the making of moonshine, but the relationship is by no means perfect. Men known to be involved in making moonshine included a part-time fisher-man and a part-time fish plant worker, several loggers who commuted back home on weekends or seasonally, two full-time fishermen, one quite successful, an employee of a utility company, and a teacher. At least half of these people were in economic situations that enabled them to pur-chase store-bought liquor at will, while for the others, the reduced cost of moonshine compared to liquor from stores was undoubtedly a major factor.

Summary

In this chapter, patterns in the consumption and production of moon-shine in the outports are described. The consumption of moonshine is affected by an outport culture in which introduction to alcohol occurs early and drinking is extensive, which suppresses labelling of heavy drinkers, yet which sanctions displays of non-utilitarian activity as indica-tors of personal laziness. Drinking moonshine occurs primarily among men in small groups, at times and in locations which shield these activ-ities from general public view. Drinking moonshine reaffirms the social relationships of those who share it. In terms of production, moonshine is manufactured by individuals for private consumption, following tradi-tional methods, in which quality is associated with alcoholic content. Just as in the past, when the unavailability of commercially manufactured liquor resulted in a general pattern of moonshine production in the outports, a significant number of those who produce their own moon-shine are heavy drinkers with limited cash resources for whom home production is probably the only means of obtaining quantities of alcohol.

8

Interpersonal Crime and Vandalism

This chapter describes incidents of interpersonal crime and vandalism, ranging from property damage and negligence to assault, including one incident of sexual assault. First, violence statistics produced by the police are examined. This is followed by a discussion of tensions and conflicts which occur in the small, face-to-face communities, and of informal social control mechanisms which limit and channel outbreaks of aggression in Newfoundland's outports. The remainder of the chapter describes incidents of fighting and assault, tormenting, and negligence and vandalism, including local perceptions of their causes and the ensuing reactions. Finally, an assessment of the effectiveness of traditional social control mechanisms in the face of the rapidly changing economic and social realities of the outports is provided.

Newfoundland Violence Statistics and Their Problems

On the basis of broad police statistics shown in tables 3.1 and 3.2, Newfoundland has the lowest rates of serious crime in the Atlantic region, which itself has the lowest regional rates of serious crime in Canada. Of particular interest for this chapter is the finding that the rate of crimes of violence in Newfoundland, while below the Canadian average, was only 20 per cent below, while reported property offences were committed at half the national rate. The suggestion that rate of violent crime in Newfoundland is relatively high for the region is bolstered by the finding that, within the Atlantic region of Canada, Newfoundland has the second highest provincial rates of assaults and sexual assaults and ranks first in juveniles charged with violence and vandalism, and in total (Smith and Kaill, 1984).

O'Grady (1986, 1989) has questioned the validity of official rates of violent crime in the Newfoundland context. His attention to statistics was the result of highly publicized increases in the violent crime rate and in retail crime in the mid-1980s and the linking of these increases to the threat to public safety posed by high levels of unemployment among youth. The resultant fear had led to calls for action by business groups, police organizations, and government bodies. On the basis of a detailed examination, O'Grady found that a jump in provincial violent crime statistics was largely the result of a change in RCMP charging practices, beginning in 1982, whereby suspects in domestic disturbances were charged with assault even though the victim often did not wish to lay charges (1986, 9). Formerly, this behaviour was reported as 'drunk and disorderly in the home,' a Liquor Control Offence classed by Statistics Canada under 'Other Provincial Statutes,' not under the Criminal Code. As a result of his analysis, O'Grady felt that there was no reason to feel that crimes of violence were increasing, or approaching 'mainland' or Canadian levels.

While the media and interest groups had selectively misinterpreted statistics to produce an inflated image of violent crime, O'Grady indicates that domestic assaults have been grossly underestimated by official statistics, owing to police desires to keep out of domestic quarrels, in the context of a patriarchal criminal justice and social setting (O'Grady, 1989).

How much, and what type, of violent activity goes on in the outports? Unfortunately, analyses done on the provincial level such as O'Grady's include St John's, the only major city in Newfoundland, and sizeable towns as well, and thus paint an unclear picture of outport crime. Further, as described in chapter 4, data based on police statistics are likely to be invalid because of the reluctance of outport residents to report crime to the police. In this chapter an attempt is made to shed some light on the nature and extent of interpersonal crime (i.e., crime which involves some sort of aggression against another person or the threat of such) and vandalism in Main Harbour and Fish Arm. The information employed in this chapter derives largely from accounts of crimes given to me by various informants. Many were dredged up from memory, but there were a few cases of interpersonal crimes which occurred while I was in the community. Because of difficulties of assigning incidents to the same categories employed by the police, no quantitative estimate of the amount of violent crime is attempted here. However, general comments on the amount of crime are offered.

Social Tensions and Social Control of Aggression in the Outports

Studies of conventional assault done in Canada and the United States portray a pattern of incidents arising out of an argument over something mundane (often over romantic entanglements), with victims and offenders disproportionately consisting of young male combatants typically known to each other (e.g., Koenig, 1987, 253–4). The outports of Newfoundland present a special case of the management of interpersonal tensions because of the visibility of behaviour (the inability to hide most behaviour) and the fact that contact between conflicting parties and their relevant kin is likely to be frequent and enduring. Fellow inhabitants of the outport are likely to remain the key figures in one's social circle for a lifetime.

Some of the tensions and conflicts that emerge in the outports are the result of values of individualism and competitiveness which have emerged. Firestone's observation of Savage Cove is instructive:

Men vie with each other for distinctions of all types from seeing who has caught the most rabbits to who can walk to the company camp the fastest ... Individuals within a crew will often compete with each other to see who jigs the most fish, and crews will compete with each other for the most fish caught in a trip or in tucking a trap ... When a crew comes in after jigging or tucking there will be inquiries from members of other crews as to the amount of the catch, and sometimes a bit of taunting by those who have done better ... Some families feel competitive about the school grades that their children receive. They are quite conscious of the class positions of their children, and this motivates them to encourage their children to do well. (1967, 125–6)

In Fish Arm and Main Harbour, this same type of competitiveness can be observed, and is often the topic of conversation. Invidious comparisons are made of a person's skill in activities such as cutting trees, building one's own house, fixing boats and nets, endurance in the outdoors, storytelling, and the ability to maintain interesting conversation for men; keeping a clean and tidy house and moral uprightness for women. In the inward-looking outports where one's daily activities are easily scrutinized and noted by everyone else, the competitive tensions remain formidable and breed envy and jealousy which challenge the informal mechanisms of social control.

As indicated in chapters 1 and 2, the principal informal social control mechanisms have been a series of rules and prescriptions which place a premium on predictable behaviour and expected response and a prohibition on overt expressions of emotion, aggression, and exploitation. The following sections describe patterns of interpersonal crime and vandalism and the social perceptions and reactions to these crimes as they are currently experienced.

Fighting and Assault

Among men, especially young men, threats of violence and actual physical assaults are rare enough that most incidents are remembered for years and become the topic of incessant conversation and gossip. As one former resident expressed it, 'The rumour mill is always going in Fish Arm.' Thus, involvement in fights can brand one deviant and induce social penalties that can make life difficult to bear for combatants who are likely to remain villagers and therefore neighbours for the duration of their lives. The expression of aggression is thus channelled into specific outlets. Drinking prior to fighting, and the fact that drinking is socially approved during 'times' and occasions, serve to deflect social criticism of individuals who get involved, allowing others to blame the events on the liquor, since the person was not 'his real self' at the time (cf. Dinham, 1977, 25; Faris, 1973, ch. 12 for a description of the reversal of roles occurring on certain 'occasions'; Chambers, 1974, 10 for a mention of fights at weddings). Thus, several people related the story of one young man in his twenties who was drinking heavily during a wedding celebration. He became verbally abusive and got in a fight in which he was knocked out by a punch thrown by someone from the village. The consensus was that the person who threw the punch was justified in doing so, and the fact that he knocked out his victim was not seen as an act of brutality but of necessity, because of the drunken behaviour of his victim. When he sobered up, the young man returned to his usual passive manner and did not attempt to retaliate against his attacker.[1]

When the target of aggression is an outsider, physical violence has fewer problematic social consequences and is tolerated more, though the perpetrators are still viewed as dangerous and unpredictable. As an example, several respondents related the story of UT, a robust young man who had developed a reputation for fighting while drinking. On one occasion, which involved competition for the attention of a local woman, he had almost 'knocked the eye out' of a person visiting from the outside, but no charges were laid and the visitor never returned to Fish Arm. The community sentiment was that 'you had to watch out for UT while he was drinking.' During a visit some years after this incident, UT related that he had indeed quit drinking, a 'fact' which was widely known through the community, no doubt in part to combat the reputation that had been acquired.[2]

The differential reaction of the community to actions committed while ostensibly under the influence of alcohol has not been lost on those who are likely to engage in aggression against others. One such person, who was seen by most as the 'nicest' or 'best sort' when sober, was seen to change completely when drunk, when he would become verbally and occasionally physically abusive to those he held grudges against. It was only when drunk, he suggested, that his real feelings came out, and furthermore, on some occasions, although people thought he was drunk out of his mind, he himself really knew what he was doing, and he claimed he always remembered what happened during his drinking.

The most serious incident of mundane assault that occurred in either outport was labelled the 'circular saw massacre' by locals (presumably after the movie *Chain Saw Massacre*). The versions vary by the teller, but the crux of the story was that the incident started with two young men who got involved in an argument at the Club (the only lounge serving liquor in town). The eventual victim started taunting the offender over a woman. The offender couldn't take it and left. The victim then went over to the offender's house (either to 'clear the air' or to beat him up, depending on who was retelling the story), where he met the offender's sister on the front porch. They had a few words. One raconteur indicated that this gave the offender time to plug in the circular saw. When the victim entered the door to the house, the offender attacked him with a circular saw. The victim somehow made it back out of the house. A couple returning from the Club saw the victim in the snow and, with the help of some others passing by, took him to the doctor's house. The doctor sent him to the hospital where sixty-seven stitches were required to close a gash near the heart. The police came to the offender's residence that night and took the offender away (presumably for questioning), but he was back home shortly. Observers noted that the offender spent almost all of his time in the period while he was awaiting trial inside his parents' house. He claimed self-defence for the attack.

It was difficult to gauge community reaction to the event, even though just a few months had lapsed when I visited the village. It is likely that the reactions of individuals to either victim or offender were not readily discerned because both combatants were from local families. Respondents clammed up or were very careful about what they said, no doubt for fear that whatever was said would become known to others. One respondent, for example, simply recited the facts of the incident when questioned and offered no opinion on guilt or sentence. Another person indicated his indirect support for the offender, noting that he knew the offender's father as a person from a neighbouring village and that he was 'all right,' but the family stuck mainly to themselves. A third observer called the offender's family 'unpredictable' and most people tried to 'stay clear' of them. At the very least, he said, the offender had the reputation of not being able to take a ribbing.

The suppression of direct expressions of opinions or statements that would label a person as criminal or deviant is an adaptive mechanism for reducing social tensions. In the tightly knit communities, public statements are likely to become known rather quickly and they can affect one's relationships with a web of other people. One example was provided by a Main Harbour man's attempt to purchase a house from a person in a nearby outport. He attempted to secure information about the seller from friends and relatives who lived in the seller's community, but the typical response was that the seller was 'perfect.' It was only when the sale fell through and the seller attempted to keep the deposit on the house that information about the seller's previous shady financial dealings was given to the victim. A more mundane example of the suppression of direct expression occurs when, in conversation, individuals are likely to verbally indicate agreement with a speaker ('yes, b'y') even if they privately disagree with him (cf. Firestone, 1967, 118).

The circular saw incident and the others that are included in this section resemble patterns of assault occurring elsewhere in North America. Young men who know each other are typically involved, often over the attentions of a woman. The overall incidence of such assaults is very low, however. If they do occur, and there is no threat to community solidarity because they occurred at appropriate times and circumstances (such as while drinking heavily at a 'time'), and there is no major injury or overt attempt to retaliate, they still become objects of rumour and gossip, so that everybody in the community can recall, often with startling clarity, their version of what happened and why. Physical fights among women are unknown, although there are some well-known feuds and much psychological and social warfare. As one outsider who had lived in the area and was a friend of the doctor noted, 'all the women are on pills' (for their nerves).

Domestic Assault

O'Grady (1989) has noted the severe under-reporting of domestic assault in the province, owing to police reluctance to record incidents brought to their attention. Getting an accurate picture of the amount and nature of domestic violence is especially difficult, if not impossible. A recent Statistics Canada Violence against Women survey (cited from Neis, 1993) found that Newfoundland had the lowest rate of violence against women in Canada, with 33 per cent of those interviewed acknowledging victimization, compared to 51 per cent for Canada as a whole. Unfortunately, this figure includes all types of violence against women, not just domestic assault. Neis (1993) notes that the social stigma attached to violence and the absence of transition houses for women in the outports leave women with few options except to leave the community. This situation contributes to potential under-reporting.

In the small outports, where people know each other intimately, where social relations with the small number of others in the village are the axis of social life, and where the huddling of houses on the limited physical space available for settlement dictates little privacy of behaviour, domestic violence is likely to be hidden from others unless it reaches a point where it cannot be hidden or is intolerable and results in the breakup of the family. Knowing that even small rifts between individuals will become grist for the rumour mill, some outport residents may strive to keep up an appearance of domestic tranquillity even with close friends and kin. Thus, one woman who was eventually separated confided that her husband had done 'everything' to her, including 'calling me everything' and engaging in physical abuse such as hitting her and pushing her around, especially when he got drunk.[3] At the time this was occurring, she said she hid it even from close family members. In two other cases described previously in this study, domestic assault was revealed only when the situation could no longer be hidden or tolerated, and in each case the minister, rather than the police, was called upon to intervene and the husband was institutionalized in a psychiatric facility.

Because of the severe social consequences that could erupt if domestic assault became known, under-reporting of this type of crime in the outports is highly likely. There are other reasons, however, for suggesting that the actual rate of domestic assault is low. As described in chapter 1, women in the outports continue to make an important economic contribution to the family, thereby reducing the potential for abuse associated with a patriarchal power structure (Beaujot in Teevan, 1992, 315). In addition, women typically maintain control over certain areas such as the house and the kitchen and generally are not oppressed or marginal to the life of the community.

The tightly knit social relations of the outport also prevent the process described by sociologists as the 'privatization of the family' (e.g., Gee in Hagedorn, 1994, 328), wherein mobile nuclear families turn inward and a person relies on the marital partner or children for emotional gratification and affection. In some cases, such a situation promotes over-dependence and violence. Women in Main Harbour and Fish Arm typically have a number of relatives and friends who are alternative sources of emotional attachment. Further, many women typically engage in female activities, both formal, such as playing in the dart league or belonging to a church group, or informal, such as helping out with a church sale or watching 'the story'[4] together. The existence of a network of kin and friendship attachments outside of marriage helps explain one of the notable peculiarities of the outports, namely the fairly large number of adults who have never married. Substitute sources of emotional attachment and meaning are available. Likewise, such community-based networks of friends and relatives act as an emotional safety net for married persons, who do not have to rely solely on spouses to satisfy emotional needs.

'Hard Tickets,' Harassment, and Tormenting

Though they generally cannot be classed as crimes, certain forms of behaviour in the outports exacerbate interpersonal tensions. Given everyone's familiarity with everyone else's personalities, personal histories, quirks, and foibles, making fun of others is possible, and a culturally accepted practice. Indeed, some outport residents achieve local prestige for their uncanny ability to imitate others, thereby providing entertainment. Others are widely known to speak what is on their minds regardless of the circumstances or who is present. They do so against the usual norms dictating conversational reserve in the communities. These people are classed as 'hard tickets' or 'hard cases.'[5] By speaking what is on their minds (and possibly on the minds of others, but unspoken), in a fashion whose main purpose is to amuse the immediate audience rather than to invoke confrontation, 'hard tickets' are not only tolerated but also accorded a strong element of respect by many. Episodes involving 'hard tickets' often become part of the folklore of the community, recitable by practically everyone.

In the case of imitation, the individual at whose expense the fun is made is not present and does not know that he or she is the target. With 'hard tickets,' however, tormenting or taunting behaviour is done with the victim present, thus skirting the local prohibitions against aggression. Verbal taunts, making fun of others while they are present, in front of an audience, make problematic the reactions of the target person and contribute to resentment, which occasionally results in overt acts of revenge. An example, adapted from field notes, will clarify:

RR was known as a 'hard ticket.' He was always poking fun at and tormenting people, including a woman, AG, who worked in a local office, and hated him for doing so. AG reputedly had gone (slept) with a man from one of the ships that stopped at Fish Arm. Of course, everyone found out about it. RR would ask her if she had any drawers on today, and worse, in front of the others in the office. At one time, an observer recalled, people at the office tried to shove him out three times (for causing trouble by tormenting AG), but RR kept coming back in saying 'What, a person can't do business here?'
  On this occasion, RR was drinking outside with a buddy when they ran out of liquor, so RR tried to get into the buddy's house to get more to drink. The screen door was locked, and in trying to get in, RR broke the latch. AG was watching all of this from her own house, and seeing the door being broken, took the opportunity to call the police. The next day, two Mounties and a justice of the peace flew in from Ruralville and the case was tried then and there. The wife of RR's buddy told the police that she did not make any complaint, and would pay for the door herself. There was no conviction, but the Mounties told RR to avoid AG, a troublemaker. (Field notes)

This event is perhaps the most dramatic example of an escalation of the frictions caused by the practice of tormenting. In tormenting, the hostility or aggression is cloaked in jest and is often quite subtle (though not in this case). The ideal outport reaction is to ignore or endure the irritation and be the 'better person' for not allowing it to bother one (cf. Firestone, 1967, 119). Because AG violated the norm of being able to 'take it' and did not retaliate in some more appropriate fashion (calling the police is considered a bald form of aggression), most community opinion sided with RR and not AG, the ostensible victim.
  Another example illustrates the elaborateness and group approval of some of these efforts at tormenting.

FV said some the guys were on the wharf drinking and throwing beer bottles into the water when they decided to play a joke on one of their members. They told one of the more gullible amongst them, KF, that they were going to go in the country that day by skidoo. He said there was 'not a flake' of snow on the ground because this was in September! KF should go get ready – buy some gas, spark plugs, and so on so they could be the first to take a snowmobile ride that season.

So KF went into the nearby store, but the store owner thought his requests were strange and wouldn't sell him any gas. KF got really 'pissed off,' saying to the crowd on the wharf (which was near the store) that the store owner wouldn't give him credit for any gas and 'I've given him every cent I ever made.' Meanwhile, the people gathered there were laughing amongst themselves. They were 'rolling on the ground' was the way FV put it. They told KF that the store owner wouldn't sell him gas because he wanted to be the first one in the country himself the next morning. Finally, some who were not as amused as the others told KF that the group was playing a joke on him and the victim went home when he realized that the others were laughing at him. (Field notes, FV)

In recent years, the advent of toll-free numbers which allow for anonymous reporting to the police or other enforcement officials has resulted in attempts to 'even the score' or help settle accounts without the social penalties which would accrue to being the known complainant. As indicated in chapter 4, calling the police was once seen as an act of overt aggression usually avoided because of the sanctions directed at the caller. It was almost unknown to call the police because of the increase in social tensions that such a call entailed. Now, calling the police or the game wardens is done with social impunity, and, given the large number of people who are in possession of illegally obtained game meat or fish, who have consumed liquor in public, or who have violated some other law, it is a mode of social revenge which has widespread applicability, particularly among young males. Indeed, anonymous calling of the police, wildlife officers, or fishery officers was being done with increasing frequency during the period of field work.

Negligence, Recklessness, and Vandalism

The prohibition on aggression limits the number of assaultive events that occur, but as indicated above, they are not unknown. Sins of omission, carelessness, and negligence, however, are harder to fault, in the outport social system. At the mundane level, simply not offering assistance (such as not offering a neighbour a ride to the post office) may be a means of social punishment, but the interaction norm is *not* to make a direct request so as to force others to accede or refuse (cf. Firestone, 1967, 129–30). A more serious example of carelessness relates to snowmobiling in the open country. Apparently, one group of snowmobilers had tied ribbons to trees in order to find their way back, while deep in the woods. Another group from the same village, coming across the ribbons, untied them 'for badness' (i.e., for no particular reason other than mischief). Only after a long period of searching was the first group able to find the way home and thereby escape the potentially fatal predicament of running out of gas and getting lost in the trackless wood, in the cold of winter.

Reckless behaviour refers to involvement in activities that have potentially dangerous consequences to oneself and possibly others. Because it involves the possibility of injury to oneself, reckless behaviour is not normally seen as aggression. However, in situations involving conflict between individuals who are very familiar with each other and where there are few other acceptable outlets for interpersonal tension, engaging in reckless behaviour is an important option. The outstanding example of recklessness which emanated from displaced aggression occurred a few months prior to my being in the field. This involved a fatal truck accident, and was described by NE, a teenage friend of most of those involved:

When I asked him what happened, he said that the driver was going about seventy miles an hour. Although the pickup truck was loaded with a fairly large number of people, the driver 'floored it' from the bend in the road at ——'s garage, and by the time they hit the turn near the take out it went off the gravel road. The driver tried to correct, but the front wheel was in the ditch, and so the truck overturned. NE said that it was lucky that they didn't hit any rocks. The only things that were nearby were a bunch of shrubs, so in a way they were lucky, but in a way they weren't. When I asked him why the driver was going so fast, he just said, 'Jealousy, I guess.' Apparently another young male was in the front seat with two girls and had his arm around both of the girls. Indeed, he was holding them, one in each arm, when they went through the windshield. The driver of the vehicle had become a little jealous because one of the girls was supposed to be 'his,' and decided to speed up the truck. The truck was, unfortunately, loaded with six or seven other teenage friends in the dump (the back), several of whom were injured seriously, and one of whom was killed. NE and his friend said that the driver had pleaded not guilty to a charge of dangerous driving in court just the other day. NE's friend commented that it wasn't right for the driver to get off, implying that if found not guilty, it wouldn't be right. (Field notes, NE)

Recklessness is one of a number of displacements for aggression. Another is cursing, or swearing, which usually is done in relation to nonhuman objects (cf. Felt, 1987). On one occasion, for example, a Fish Arm man's boat motor stopped shortly after he had left the dock for a pleasure cruise. This resulted in an uninterrupted string of heartfelt curses lasting for several minutes, including a spirited repetition of phrases taking the Lord's name in vain. Another Fish Arm man's snowmobile stalled out just as he was about to embark on a long winter trip with two companions, who had already left. While he worked to get the snowmobile started, he invoked the names of a large number of Christian religious figures, interspersing them with comments like 'this Jesus machine won't be with me come the fall.'

Vandalism is less frequent than one may think, largely because of the visibility of behaviour. That is, it is a relatively easy matter to trace the culprits, given the intimate knowledge everyone has of everyone else's activity patterns and likely motivations. As one respondent put it, 'You can't get away with anything here.' An example of this was the case of a snowmobile that was determined to be missing one morning. OF, the owner, asked a relative to help locate it and they eventually found it, out of gas and with a damaged windshield and cab. Since OF lived near the Club, he phoned the owner and found out who were the last to leave the night before. The last person to leave the Club was a known troublemaker, so it was easy for the police to get a confession.

Vandalism involving the property of people who are not members of the local community seems to be the rule. One example involved an outsider who built a home in a community neighbouring Main Harbour, but who eventually became ostracized by the community. While he was on vacation out of the country, his boat was smashed and he had difficulty getting anyone to rent or buy his house. Similarly, as mentioned in chapter 5, the cabins of the game warden for Fish Arm were damaged on several occasions.

The Social Penalization of Deviants

It is clear from the field work that practically all serious infractions of the law become known to at least some members of the community, and such infractions are often the subject of news and gossip even if they are not reported to the police. It is also clear that there is almost no stranger-committed crime because there are few strangers and anyone new in these isolated settlements quickly becomes the focus of curiosity and concern. For those who are or aspire to become full members of the moral community (cf. Faris, 1973), the social penalties associated with violating norms of interaction are severe and have effectively inhibited actual physical aggression, except in the stylized and channelled occasions and circumstances (e.g., while drinking) indicated above. Social exclusion from the community is the ultimate punishment. Even for outsiders, these penalties are effective. Thus an older man who moved into the area and hung around with locals but who violated local norms by making passes at local married women and by exploiting a known alcoholic, enticing him to build his house without payment except for beer, complained to me (another presumably sympathetic outsider) that the community let him in and then dropped him 'just like that.' He shortly afterwards left the community.

For those who 'belong to' the community, the inhibition against the expression of aggression includes a reluctance to label individuals as criminal in spite of their engagement in behaviour that violates the law. Attributing the incident to drinking (see chapter 7) or to 'bad nerves' serves to excuse the behaviour and allow the individual to remain part of the moral community. Only when the behaviour or the person is seen as quite problematic, dangerous, or unpredictable will there be attempts to remove him or her from the community (cf. Dinham, 1977, for the case of mental illness), and this is usually done through an intermediary, a professional such as a doctor, minister, or social worker. Thus, a notorious Main Harbour heavy drinker was tolerated until he physically abused his wife, at which point he was taken from the community by the police. Eventually he wound up in the provincial mental institution.

Repeat Offenders

During the period of field work in Main Harbour, there were three young men who 'hung around' together (they formed a 'crowd'). These men were involved in most of the recent 'major' crime reported to the police in the community. One or more of them were involved in crimes which included theft of liquor and cigarettes, clothes, and gasoline, and the snowmobile theft incident described above in chapter 3. All three of them had served, or were serving, time in jail, or were jailed during the research period. They form an interesting set of cases, since they have continued to reside in Main Harbour and thus provide an opportunity to examine the strength of social control processes now operating there.

In his examination of the continuance of deviance among young male property offenders incarcerated in St John's prison, Stebbins (1971) indicates some of the social penalties that the community exacts upon ex-prisoners: for example, staring, humiliating remarks, questioning aspects of the morality of their behaviour, and so on. These penalties inhibit their rehabilitation in the community. Of the ten in his sample who were from villages of less than 7499, many reported that their reputation had spread beyond their home town to neighbouring villages (129).

It is certainly true that the three repeat offenders are known throughout the region and to the police as well (interview with Constable Y). Since they have all been in jail for known local crimes and they come from marginal families, Main Harbour residents were more open in airing their private views about the three repeat offenders than might have been expected, given the practice of cautiousness in outport interaction. Thus, a prominent local citizen took pains to assure me that the individuals' families had moved in from somewhere else and did not belong to the community. A teenaged resident who knew one of the trio quite well labelled him as lazy, noting that while in jail he was forced to clear trees and he 'wouldn't be liking that.' Another older male resident said that one offender, DQ, was 'the nicest kind of guy, he'd do anything for you. If you wanted something from him, he'd give it to you with a smile on his face, but at the same time he goes around stealing. That's not the sort of people I want to hang around with' (field notes, OF).

The inhibition of aggression in public interaction led to some peculiar situations when direct conversation with one of the three labelled youths occurred. Thus, DQ was picked up, while hitchhiking back to Main Harbour from jail, by a person who did not know he had been imprisoned. When asked, in passing, what he had been doing, DQ replied with complete candour that he had just got out of jail, and that it was a 'perfect' place – good food and so on. The only thing wrong with it was there was no beer (field notes, OF). On other occasions, knowing the likely passive or impassive reaction of other, FS (another of the offenders) would say to his peers, 'Someone broke into such and such a place' or 'Someone stole some gasoline last night' when, in fact, the perpetrator was himself.

The inhibition of aggression even against repeat offenders makes clear the limits of the effectiveness of informal social controls. For such controls to work, individuals must be part of the moral community.[6] Perhaps the most significant indicator that informal social control mechanisms on persons marginal to moral community are ultimately futile was the fact that one of the three young men was charged with sexual assault after raping a local woman. Unfortunately, I have little good data on community reactions to this event, but this case is the first reported sexual assault mentioned by anyone in either community.

Conclusion

The physical and social intimacy of outport life and the values of individualism and competitiveness result in interpersonal tensions that could lead to overt aggression and crime were it not for informal social control mechanisms inhibiting and channelling aggression. Incidents of fighting and assault are still rare and, as noted in the 'classic' outport literature, tend to occur during 'times' or occasions such as weddings where 'reversals' of usual behaviour are acceptable and heavy drinking provides an excuse. Other culturally supported modes of expressing interpersonal enmity include tormenting and taunting, which stops short of physical action; negligence and carelessness, which, by being passive adaptations, hold the perpetrator blameless and thus do not carry the stigma of aggression; and recklessness, where it is not clear that the action is directed against someone else. Vandalism is infrequent unless the target is an outsider. Domestic assaults are rarely revealed even to close kin or friends until they can no longer be tolerated or hidden. Even then, the perpetrators are more likely to be classed as suffering from psychiatric problems than to be jailed.

As in other parts of North America, most overt acts of interpersonal violence are carried out by young males.[7] The fact that most of these acts occur in the context of drinking, particularly during 'times,' is an indication of the effectiveness of informal social control mechanisms. The limits of the effectiveness of informal social control, however, are clearly demonstrated in the case of repeat offenders. The inhibition of interpersonal aggression and tolerance by others have worked in their favour, resulting in a situation of completely inadequate social deterrence, with predictable results. Their removal from the community will likely be through the process of the formal justice system.

A comparison between Fish Arm and Main Harbour is instructive in that Fish Arm is much more isolated and probably more typical of the outports in previous decades. Importantly, there has been no emergence of a criminally oriented 'crowd' in Fish Arm. Informal social control mechanisms seem more effective because of the isolation of the community. This isolation has resulted in insulation from other facets of the larger society as well, including drugs like marijuana, the use of which has been 'marked' or noted by several observers in Main Harbour.

In this chapter the focus has been on interpersonal crime and its causes. Interpersonal crime needs to be understood in the context of social relationships and interaction patterns in isolated outports. Unlike the often fleeting, segmented, and secondary relationships which characterize life in many urban areas, interaction between familiars forms the axis of outport social life.[8] There is a tremendous richness and complexity in the interaction among people intimately known to each other and thus treated as unique individuals. People are reacted to, talked about, and treated on the basis of personalities, quirks, traits, personal styles, character strengths and flaws, past interaction experiences, kinship ties, and family histories. While it is true that the outport values like competitiveness and individualism fan jealousies and tensions between individuals, informal social control mechanisms, including the inhibition and channelling of verbal and especially physical aggression, tolerance by others, and the reluctance to label, remain remarkably effective.

9

Crimes of the Powerful

One of the central themes in studies of Newfoundland life is the unchecked exploitation of the masses by the few in positions of power.[1] An historical treatment of some political and economic dimensions of this theme was offered in chapter 2. The goal of this chapter is to describe patterns of behaviour that are manifestations of the severe economic and social inequalities in the outports in the past two or three decades. Also described are the cultural modes of acquiescence among the powerless, deference to authority and submission, which have helped maintain such inequalities.

It is important to note that many of the incidents and patterns recounted below are not criminal, though some clearly do violate laws. None of these incidents have been reported to the police. I have labelled them as 'crimes of the powerful' (cf. 'crimes of domination' described by Quinney, 1979) in recognition of the unequal distribution of power and influence among groups, collectivities, or classes (for the Canadian context, see, for example, Fleming, 1985, and Ratner, 1985), a situation that results in selective passage and enforcement of laws favouring the interests of the more powerful. In the outport context, the classification of powerful people includes outside professionals who reside in the village and perform important services, such as the doctor, nurse, and minister, and, to a lesser extent, the teachers. The police, though not stationed in either Main Harbour or Fish Arm, are also included. The local fish plant operator (who is often also a dominant merchant), however, is far and away the most important and powerful figure in the outports, and the bulk of the incidents described in this chapter involve domination and exploitation by the plant operator.

The sources of information are people's accounts of incidents, some of which occurred some time ago, and first-hand observation by the author.

Academic Treatment of the Economic Subjugation of Outport Fishermen

At a macro level, there are a number of studies that have dealt with the economic plight of the people from the remote fishing villages of Newfoundland. Most of these studies focus on the fishing industry. Typically, a report or study will provide a lengthy economic analysis of fishery-related problems, such as variable catches and low fish prices affecting the inshore fishery, and then briefly discuss the general impact of these problems on local people. The studies associated with economic underdevelopment literature in Atlantic Canada clearly fit this pattern. Government-commissioned reports and studies, usually generated because of a crisis in the fishery, make up the bulk of the post-Confederation research (see Hinds, 1995, 271 for a partial list of important studies). Until 1970, the main thrust of recommendations was to encourage the growth of Newfoundland into a modern monetary economy (providing justification for the resettlement program and government attempts to promote industry), thereby reducing its dependence on the fishery. The failure of these diversification strategies has resulted in two newer approaches. The first has been to recommend reduction in the number of people involved in the fishery. Along this line, the suggestions have ranged from the politically unfeasible position of simply depopulating the province advocated by Copes (1972) to an elimination of programs that have made the fishery an 'employer of last resort,' thereby making possible a reasonable living for a smaller number of full-time fishermen (e.g., Schrank et al., 1992). The second involves a 'small is beautiful' approach (Overton, 1990). Government policies are to be aimed at fostering self-reliance and encouraging small-scale business so as to reduce dependency on government and help sustain life in the outports (e.g., House et al., 1989). This entails, among other options, favouring the inshore segment vis-à-vis the offshore in fish quota schemes (e.g., Sinclair, 1990). In all of this work, it is assumed that the outport resident is simply the pawn of wider economic forces, which is, of course, true. What is missing from these studies is a description of the way in which these macro-economic realities have been translated into micro-level behaviour among individuals in the outports.

A small but important branch of the literature on underdevelopment in Atlantic Canada, which uses a political economy or Marxist perspective (see especially articles in Brym and Sacouman, 1979, and Fairley et al., 1990), provides a more explicit treatment of how people in fishing villages have reacted to broad economic change. The Marxist literature documents the way in which corporate capital interests, with the assistance of government loans and government policies that encouraged their growth, have come to dominate the Atlantic ground fish industry through the use of capital-intensive offshore trawlers and factory ships and larger plants (e.g., Neis, 1991). Researchers using this paradigm have documented collective local responses like unionization (Williams and Theriault, 1990) and civil disobedience and resistance to government policies and their enforcement (Grady and Sacouman, 1990). While many fishermen in Newfoundland have become unionized, there has been little evidence of collective resistance to domination or increasing political power (e.g., Brox, 1972, 182; Sider, 1986, 184; Neis, 1991).

Anthropological and sociological studies carried out in the 'golden age' of outport research (see chapters 1 and 2) suggest that the lack of effective collective responses to forces threatening the livelihood of fishermen was rooted in the culture of the outport, and particularly in patterns of domination and submission. Sider described such patterns as they existed at the time of the traditional salt cod fishery:

For the century or more that the village fishery predominated (approximately 1830–1960), Newfoundland fisher families, like North American tribes people producing fur or deerskins in a colonial context, sold the product of their labour, not their labour itself. They were constrained to produce a very specific saleable commodity (for Newfoundlanders this was 'light-salted, hard-dried' codfish) in as large a quantity as possible. Such constraints were twofold: the specific and focused suppression of viable alternatives to producing one or a very few specific commodities, which defined what they would do, and the severe disadvantages that they suffered in terms of trade for supplies that became necessities, which defined how hard they would do it.

The domination that fisher families encountered was so severe that it permeated all other aspects of their social life. It shaped the outlines of their economic activities, keeping them poor and their equipment small-scale, and thus limiting the size of the potential catch. Moreover, the specific forms that domination took introduced specific competitive tensions within villages and families that played a key role in the shaping of village family life and village culture. Yet for all the constraints and pressures that pervaded and shaped much of their social life, fisher families controlled their own social relations of work, built and owned their productive equipment, and wove the various threads of self-determination within the fabric of their social life, alongside and crossing the strands of imposed poverty and need. The domination that outport people faced occurred at the point of exchange, not production, and thus despite its severity the fishing villages retained a certain autonomy, partial but crucial. (Sider, 1986, 27–8)

As noted in chapter 1, in spite of marked change in the Newfoundland outport fishery, the domination of the exchange relationship between fishermen and fish buyers or plant owners has not changed much. In both Fish Arm and Main Harbour, fishermen are still tied into selling their fish to the local plant because of the necessity of immediately processing sometimes large quantities of fresh fish before they spoil, which limits how far one can travel by boat. Small-boat fishermen, especially, cannot travel daily during the fishing season to get their catch to another fish plant. Even for long liner owners, the closest competitor to the local fish plant is many hours away by boat, and Northern Bay is often rough during the fishing season, making regular travel unfeasible.[2] The individual local fisherman seeking an alternative to selling to the local fish buyer or plant must also face the potentially serious penalties that might be incurred by alienating the local fish plant operator, who, by virtue of others' dependence on him, could cause economic and social grief to the recalcitrant individual.[3] The dependence of fishermen on 'stamps' obtained from official fish buyers documenting the sale of fish in order to maintain eligibility for unemployment insurance benefits during the off-season has consolidated the economic power of the dominant fish buyers.

Patterns of Dominance of Fishermen

A number of local practices were observed which continue to favour the fish plant operator or fish buyer in dealings with fishermen. Determination of fish prices, for example, is partly dependent on quality, which is judged by the buyer. In the case of salmon, which are caught by gill net, even fish with small 'net burns' or bruises are classed as 'number two,' and fetch much lower prices.[4] The grumbles of the affected fishermen and occasional disbelieving looks at wharf-side testify to disenchantment with what is viewed as unfair classification, though rarely is anything overtly said. Sometimes a fisherman will take a 'number two' salmon home for family consumption rather than accept a low price for it.

In Fish Arm, even with the advent of a community-built fish plant managed by the dominant merchant, fishermen until quite recently still only received credits, which are generally used only at the dominant merchant's store. By controlling, to the extent that he could,[5] the price of fish and the price of supplies and groceries, the merchant has kept the unequal economic relationship between the parties remarkably intact, with predictable consequences. One middle-aged woman, for example, recalled that her father, having had a good year 'at the fish' in the mid 1970s, was expecting to clear the accumulated debts from his account and to have enough credit left over to buy a new motor for his boat. Not only did this not happen during that year, the debts were never cleared and the surplus never accumulated during the father's lifetime.[6]

In the past, the impoverishing effect of the cashless 'credit' system was exacerbated by the fact that few, if any, people kept track of what they owed. The record of debts incurred and credits for fish (the books) were kept by the merchant. A retired fisherman suggested that these records were sometimes manipulated to the benefit of the merchant, offering as evidence the fact that a local person who was hired to help keep the books some years previously had quit because a member of the merchant's family was adding entries to fishermen's accounts for goods which the fishermen never received. People's general tendency not to maintain their own separate records of transactions with the merchant (partly as an indication of trust and loyalty) rendered it difficult to ascertain the extent to which wrongdoing had taken place. It is still true today that many small-boat fishermen do not keep records of their catches, or their purchases from the merchant. Thus, one such individual estimated that he had paid 'three times what I owed' for a snowmobile bought from the merchant.

With little or no duplicate documentation, the status of transactions which occur between merchant and fisherman sometimes becomes a matter of opinion. In this regard, the plant owner/merchant's public pronouncements can be completely at odds with fishermen's views, and in all likelihood will prevail among people who count. For example, an outside professional who took a position in one of the communities studied was told by one merchant that the people owed him 'one hundred thousand dollars' in debts which he could not collect. When this figure was mentioned to a long-time resident, the fisherman became very agitated, saying that if the people owed a hundred thousand dollars, the merchant owed them 'at least a million' and that he had 'robbed the people blind.'

In part, the continued domination by the fish buyer/merchant is a function of past economic success, continuing enterprise, and others' resignation to the difficulty of changing things. One relatively successful fisherman, for example, relayed his experiences of contacting a kinsman living in a city to try to obtain special-sized nets for a species of fish which had just come into local waters. After several phone calls, the relative found out that these nets were available only from a company in Scandinavia, and that the company's entire stock on hand had been purchased hours before by a Northern Bay merchant! When he found out about this, the fisherman commented on the futility of further attempts to obtain his own fishing supplies.

The Fish Plant

The power differential between the select few and the others is clearest in the fish plant. Employees are drawn from a more or less captive village population and must receive at least ten weeks of employment to be eligible for unemployment insurance benefits for the rest of the year.[7] Wages are low, with workers getting about $5.00 per hour with no provision for increased pay for overtime. There are no apparent fringe benefits other than eligibility for unemployment insurance. In one of the plants in the research area, sweat-shop conditions clearly operated. Talking was not permitted, and breaks were short, barely offering enough time to eat. The workers were exhorted to work as hard as they could and did so, in spite of the fact that the harder they worked, the fewer hours they were paid for. When the fish came in, the plant workers put in as much as eighteen hours at a stretch. One worker reputedly worked ninety-four hours during an especially busy week.

Management-worker relations reflect the powerlessness of the workers. For example, on one occasion, I was standing on a fish plant wharf, watching as plant workers were unloading cod from a long liner. The fish were taken from the boat in plastic tubs which, being full, were quite heavy, requiring that several men take turns lifting them from the ship up to the wharf. Suddenly, the plant manager, who was observing the activity, turned on one of the fish plant workers and started yelling at him for being 'too lazy to work' and at one point even began pushing and shoving him to get him to move faster. This abusive behaviour kept up for a few minutes, in full public view of at least a dozen people who had gathered to watch the fish being unloaded. Later conversations with villagers, some of whom worked in the fish plant, brought forth a reluctant acknowledgment that management was dictatorial and that working conditions in the fish plant were geared to get the maximum productivity with little consideration for the workers. The general attitude, however, was resignation to the fact that this was the way it was here. After all, there was only one industry – the fishery – and one fish plant which provided almost all the paid employment to be had in the village. That a similar situation existed in a fish plant owned by an outside firm (though managed locally) was indicated by the comments of a young man seasonally employed in it: 'I thought slavery went out a long time ago.'

Such working conditions can only occur among a population with no alternatives, and ultimately who allow it. In the outports of Newfoundland, the value of hard work and the sanctions visited upon those who are deemed to be 'lazy,' combined with an emphasis on interpersonal competition, support such a situation, a fact that is exploited by the fish plant operators.[8] Thus, an older female fish plant worker admiringly described the ability of one worker to fillet five or six hundred pounds of fish per hour, though the minimum requirement for being hired was to fillet only 130 pounds in an hour. Plant workers are also proud of their reputation for being able to process large amounts of fish more quickly than plants in other villages in Newfoundland.

Sharp Dealings

People related stories of sharp dealings by those in positions of economic power which skirt laws and regulations. An older person related, for example, that one merchant had in the past received government reimbursement for clothing and food which he had supposedly given to needy families, but which were either never received by those families or for which his reimbursement was grossly inflated. This was made easier because the government welfare officer apparently spent most of the little time he was in the community in the merchant's office. In another case, which was reiterated by several people, a family whose house had burned down reportedly received a box of clothing as a 'donation' from the merchant. Upon opening the package, they found 'all the old clothing that they couldn't sell in the store.' In spite of the fact that 'half of it was "in flitters" (falling apart),' the merchant reputedly received reimbursement from the Red Cross for this contribution.

A more recent story of 'sharp' practices involved a local 'hard ticket' who, on an open line radio show, reportedly complained about the inflated price of beer charged by the only store in the village that had a licence to sell liquor and beer. He thought (validly) that beer prices were supposed to be set at the same level throughout the province. In spite of this public allegation, no investigation took place, nor were charges laid. Another sharp practice was revealed by a person who, according to the information, was resentful of the way in which a local government position, which was passed down through families and had a small monthly stipend attached to it, ended up in the hands of a member of the plant operator's family. The incumbent had promised to pass the position to someone else, but changed his/her mind at the last moment when visited by the plant owner on his/her death-bed.

Differential Contact with Influential Outsiders

Much of the success of plant operator/merchant families in maintaining their economic dominance can be traced to their ability to control contact with influential outsiders. Non-resident outside professionals such as the police, social workers, representatives of provincial and federal government programs, and the occasional visiting politician invariably meet members of the dominant families and sometimes few others. In both Main Harbour and Fish Arm, the owners of the dominant businesses were outgoing and pleasant, and especially helpful to outsiders. In the absence of any other local political leaders,[9] and given the reluctance of ordinary outport citizens to seek local leadership positions because this would violate norms of equality (cf. Porter, 1982), the word of the plant operator/merchant carries inordinate weight.

Differential contact and influence with government officials appear to play an important role in obtaining government contracts and funding. Federal government programs such as the Atlantic Canada Opportunities Agency (ACOA, now defunct) and similar provincial programs aimed at helping local businesses to start and/or expand seem to have differentially gone to economically or socially prominent community members. In Fish Arm, for example, the largest grant in recent years went to a member of the dominant merchant's family to build and operate a tourist facility.[10] Members of this same family run the fish plant, operate the postal delivery service, teach at a local school, have obtained lucrative fishing licences, and have been hired to teach under a fishermen's retraining program. Likewise, members of a school principal's family have been successful in getting a number of government grants.

In addition to their contacts and influence with powerful outsiders, local dominant family members are much more likely than others in the outport to request or employ the services of outside professionals. Chapter 4 describes how most outport residents are reluctant to report others to the police for fear of social sanctions, but it was also noted that the medical practitioners and the merchants' families are less affected by this pressure. One merchant, for example, went so far as to employ the services of a law firm to collect a debt owed by someone who had moved to another province. In this case, the merchant's lawyer had a summons issued and successfully brought to court and garnisheed the wages of the ex-resident. This differential use of and access to outside professional services have undoubtedly increased the gulf between the powerful families and others in the communities who generally are unfamiliar with, reluctant to use, and/or unable to afford these services.

General Deference to Authority

One of the most noteworthy features of Main Harbour and Fish Arm life is the way in which outside professionals holding official positions of power are accorded respect and are treated with deference that in some cases borders on outright submission. The doctor or the resident nurse, the minister, and to a lesser extent the teacher all provide desired services and, given the difficulty of attracting and retaining such persons in small, isolated communities with few cultural attractions and relatively low salaries compared to similar positions elsewhere, there is a collective local effort to provide additional social and economic rewards to such persons. Thus, a number of people in Fish Arm, wishing to retain the nurse, provided grass and hay for her horse and put up with its propensity to bite anyone who ventured too close to its fenced enclosure, which was next to the only road in the settlement (field notes, MW). On the occasions of his winter visits, the minister is carried around by snowmobile or given the use of someone's machine and stays at different houses for meals. In a similar fashion, as mentioned before, a Main Harbour woman, explaining why she did not complain about being forced to wait for a long time while the doctor, in plain view, took inventory at an apparently leisurely pace, said she did not complain because she did not want to be a cause of the doctor's leaving.

The acquiescence of the villagers is not limited to outside professionals. One informant suggested that the family who owned the main store and the fish plant in his community often made demands of people 'as if they were royalty.' In the past, it was common for children passing their house to be beckoned to come in and help with household chores.[11] Even today, some women are occasionally 'asked' to knit an artifact, or young men are asked to help around the merchant's stores, all without remuneration. This was not so much a polite request for a favour as it was a routine requisition of services, denial of which could threaten the good will of the plant operator/merchant. Because of the dependency of fishing families on jobs in the fish plant and sometimes for credit at the store, the loss of such good will could not be lightly considered.

Economic dependence on the good will of the fish plant operator/ merchant by individual families is the basis for the unreciprocated requisition of services. When this dependence is removed, individual responses are often different. Thus, one man who had moved away from the area was asked, on visiting his home community, to help move some boxes on the wharf near the merchant's store. His reply to the merchant indicated a long-standing resentment against this sort of request: 'I'm not getting paid to do that. Get one of your lackeys [paid employees] to do it.'

Crimes by Agents of Social Control

In chapter 4, an incident was described in which a group of police and wildlife officers conducted a village-wide search for poached moose meat in Fish Arm, cavalierly entering the premises of citizens. While this incident was probably the most dramatic example, there have been a number of incidents in which agents of social control seem to have ignored individual rights and gone beyond ordinary measures in their policing of outport residents. Following Quinney (1979), I label these incidents crimes of social control. Searches and seizures of items by law enforcement officials pursuing violations of hunting or fishing regulations probably constitute the most common such incidents in the outports. Chapter 10 provides further examples of searches and surveillance which amount to harassment of outport citizens.

Crimes by agents of social control are not limited to hunting and gathering situations. The following 1970s incident was recounted independently by several respondents. Apparently, someone had called the police because of the problem of dogs roaming the village. At that time, many families kept large sled dogs for hauling wood around. The Mountie who came into the village pulled out his gun and, walking down the road, shot twelve or thirteen dogs on sight, including one that was tied up. This particular dog hid under a porch, but it was so badly wounded that the owner had to put it out of its misery anyway. The owner's son, who was around thirteen at the time, witnessed the incident and swore he would 'get' the 'son-of-a-bitch Mountie' who had shot his dog. Although no one took any further action, the incident was not forgotten, as the son happily related that he had heard that this one cop had been kicked out of the force and jailed some years later.

The two incidents referred to above indicate that, in comparison to urban experience, the police do not appear to be much concerned with the preservation of individual rights or restraining their own behaviour. This seems particularly true given the triviality of the offences that typically concern the police when they come into Main Harbour or Fish Arm: poaching or possession of poached moose or caribou meat; dogs running loose; drinking in public or serving alcohol to minors.

It is not that the police action in these situations goes beyond the scope of their legitimate powers. The powers given to police officers in Canada are very broad, particularly the powers of search that were given some RCMP officers under 'writs of assistance,' which were essentially *carte blanche* search warrants (Griffiths et al., 1980). In addition, the Wildlife Act of Newfoundland appears to give very broad powers of search and seizure to game wardens in the province (Newfoundland and Labrador, 1982). How these broad powers are used, however, is the result of police discretion in opting to carry out their duties in a particular fashion. What are the factors that influence law enforcement officers to select one course of action among the many possibilities?

The difficulty and cost of policing isolated, small communities like Main Harbour and Fish Arm were discussed in chapter 3. Police contacts are infrequent, usually result in trouble for someone locally, and are quickly communicated across the village. Culturally induced submission to and fear of the police in the outports are heightened by the 'legalistic' style of policing associated with the RCMP (Wilson, 1968). Officers are recruited not locally but in a bureaucratic fashion, are highly trained and are expected to remain detached from the community and enforce the laws impersonally. In Atlantic Canada, there is a high turnover rate in rural detachments (Perrier, n.d.), making it even less likely that individual police officers will develop a detailed knowledge of the people in their jurisdiction. Police officers remain strangers, thus reinforcing the perception of them as threatening outsiders. In their occasional visits, then, perhaps the major resource that Mounties bring with them is the Mountie image, respect and fear of which is probably increased by their connection with the powerful federal government and by the vast resources which they command, including the use of helicopters and other equipment in mass raids.

From the point of view of the local detachment, a police officer's visit to an isolated outport in the winter entails a commitment of at least the better part of a whole day and perhaps the considerable expense of flying in and out of the community. Thus, it is likely that there will be some pressure on officers to show some concrete result in the form of an arrest or summons. The greater the investment of police resources, as in larger-scale search efforts, the greater the pressure to show such results, even at the expense, one presumes, of some violation of individual rights.

The Subjective Warrant of Law Enforcement Officers

The way a given group is policed, both by individual officers and by departments and precincts as a general strategy, is affected by police perceptions of the likely consequences of their actions (Chambliss and Seidman, 1971). As indicated in chapter 4, in the outports, the typical reaction to contact with law enforcement officials is an unquestioning submission often tinged with fear. Local residents may feel harassed, and resent treatment at the hands of law enforcement officials, but rarely is this resentment reflected in outright protest or other overt instrumental action other than local talk. These culturally ingrained attitudes to authority probably give officers a wide subjective warrant or licence (cf. Lortie, 1975). Thus, knowing or sensing that outport residents are unlikely to do much about police actions which in other areas would result in some sort of legal recourse, media outcry, or political reaction, the police are free to conduct massive search raids, to 'lord it' over locals. They feel freer to engage in actions that show little concern for outport residents' rights, and to engage in behaviour aimed at keeping in check a powerless and fearful populace, a populace with no tradition of self-rule or individual rights.

   A number of incidents indicated that, while the extreme examples given above have not recently been repeated, cavalier treatment of outport people by law enforcement officials still occurs. One Fish Arm respondent described how, upon being called to investigate a claim that underage teens were served alcoholic beverages, the RCMP officers who came to the village simply ordered those thought to be involved (mostly teens and young adults) to come into a room in a merchant's store, for individual questioning. These people were told that the police already knew who had supplied the liquor, and it was made clear that less than full co-operation would be dealt with severely. There was no communication of information about rights to a lawyer, rights regarding self-incrimination, and so on. Similarly, snowmobile riders are still frequently and arbitrarily stopped and their machines and equipment searched, often very thoroughly. As indicated in chapter 5, homes and vehicles also continue to be searched, often on the basis of an anonymous and perhaps groundless tip.

There was some indication that police-citizen interaction was changing, at least in terms of the balder violations of citizen rights. Thus, a local judge indicated that the days when the RCMP came in and just shot dogs were a thing of the past. 'The Mounties want to protect their own skins so they don't do that sort of thing anymore, and it's different among the younger generation anyhow' (field notes, Judge O).

The subjective warrant or perceived licence to enforce the laws as one pleases is not available to fishery officers or game wardens. These enforcement officials are residents either of the local community or of one nearby. As such, they are members of the moral community of the village. Enforcing regulations against another local person violates the prohibition against aggression towards fellow residents. The best example of the strength of the prohibition against aggression was told by an older fisherman. It involved a Fish Arm man who was appointed a game warden some decades ago. On one occasion, the fisherman and two companions had just illegally killed a deer and quartered it. They were coming down a path to the village when one of the companions saw snowshoe tracks, some of which he recognized as those of the game warden. The companion became 'frightened to death.' 'Yes,' he said, 'that's the warden and he has somebody else with him. We're gone now. We might as well give up.' The other two men sat down and 'killed themselves laughing': they knew the game warden had taken the job because he was on welfare at the time and 'only did it for the money.' The warden apparently never went beyond the ridge behind his house to search for poachers and would turn a blind eye to even flagrant violations of hunting regulations, because he was 'afraid of bad feelings between neighbours' (field notes, SL).

That fishery officers and game wardens are treated in part on the basis of outport norms and values is indicated by more recent examples where local officials have attempted to enforce regulations against local offenders. Thus, the Fish Arm fisherman who barred a game warden from entering his house to search did not bar the RCMP officer(s) who accompanied him. In another recent incident in Main Harbour, a locally recruited fishery officer was slapped by another resident who was unhappy with being caught.

Conflict between members of the community and game wardens or fishery officers is kept to a minimum by a number of devices. The number of incidents which result in being caught is small. This is the result of inability to keep one's behaviour secret in the small, intimate outport, and the reluctance of most officers to aggressively pursue offenders. A local fishery officer explained that his job involves checking out complaints and reports of illegal fishing that come in. People will call and report that someone is fishing in a certain spot and when they see him going up the road to check it out, they go somewhere else and poach fish. They know his main job is to keep an eye out on the —— River and they also know his routine, including when his eight-hour shift begins and ends. They set out their illegal salmon nets between eleven (at night) and five (in the morning), staying out to pick them (collect the fish) and then take them away. They know that he does not get paid for overtime and is 'not going to go out and stay later' (field notes, GV).

The fact that, while on the job, fishery officers and game wardens wear distinctive clothing or uniforms also serves the important function of distinguishing for all the behaviour of the person from his duties as an enforcement official. This serves to depersonalize interactions between enforcers and offenders and give support to the attitude that, as one known poacher put it, 'somebody has to do the job.'

Some government departments have recognized the conflict caused by having local enforcement officers deal with local violators. One strategy developed by the Department of Wildlife and Recreation to reduce this conflict is to try to change outport attitudes. This they attempted to do by engaging in a public relations campaign designed to make people more aware of the necessity of conservation. A regional supervisor indicated that he gave presentations to organizations four or five times a month and often went into schools. By talking to younger people, those in grade 10 or 11, he hoped he would be able to influence the older people as well, because 'if the father was a poacher, the son would be one too.' A more dramatic educational strategy was taken by a game warden who snowmobiled throughout Fish Arm on one occasion displaying the unused remains of several moose, including cows with calves, which had been needlessly slaughtered nearby.

These attempts to change outport cultural attitudes towards the enforcement of hunting regulations have had some impact. Thus, one fisherman who had been a notorious poacher in earlier days described how 'the wildlife people put four female caribou and one stag on an island some distance away in Northern Bay.' Ten years later, he indicated, there were four hundred caribou, and shortly before the research period of this study, there were so many that hunting licences had been issued to people as far away as Fish Arm. These hunts were supervised, with game wardens accompanying the hunters. The fisherman concluded by saying that he now supported the enforcement of wildlife regulations and that 'it was an amazing thing you can do with conservation' (field notes, BI).

While there was some evidence that, in the area of wildlife, officials were succeeding in raising the awareness of outport residents about game issues and thus reducing friction between game wardens and outport residents, chapter 10 indicates that, in the crucial economic area of the fishery, the Department of Fisheries and Oceans has faced a much more serious challenge to its policies and their enforcement.

10

Government Policy and Social Order in a Collapsed Economy

In the preceding chapters, the major argument has been that patterns of crime in the outports have been affected by their unique social arrangements and culture, a culture that has emerged out of a peculiar adaptation to geographical constraints and economic history. The complete collapse of the fishery and the subsequent moratorium on commercial fishing for ground fish in 1992 (described briefly in chapter 2) have drastically affected life in the outports. The goal of this chapter is to describe the present and suggest the future near-term impact on crime and social order of the catastrophic economic changes that have befallen Newfoundland, and that promise to be more than temporary. The chapter begins with a summary of events in the Atlantic fishery that led to the collapse of the cod stocks, and a description of the government policies for dealing with the economic catastrophe. An examination of the immediate impact of these events on the daily lives of outport residents follows. The remainder of the chapter provides an analysis of the potentially criminogenic impact of the economic downturn and subsequent government policy on the mode of life in rural Newfoundland. This includes a description of changes in regulations of the inshore fishery by the Department of Fisheries and Oceans that have exacerbated tensions within communities and heightened the levels of social and economic stratification. Also examined are changes in life style brought about by the forced idling of whole communities of individuals, and the criminalization of activities associated with traditional outport modes of subsistence. The latter has been caused by the government's declaration and enforcement of a complete moratorium on fishing, even for family consumption, and the increasing regulation and enforcement of traditional hunting and gathering activities. The chapter ends with an assessment and prognosis about the extent and types of crime and collective unrest that are likely to emerge in the outports during the new 'hard times,' and with some suggestions for preventing them.

The Collapse of the Cod Stocks

The government's first inkling that there were major problems with the Newfoundland cod stocks came in 1989 when biomass estimates were dramatically below previous levels (Meltzer, 1994). The ensuing alarm resulted in the president of Memorial University being asked to conduct an independent review of scientists' recommendations in regard to cod stocks. Meanwhile, the low catches caused fish plants to close. In the summer of 1990, the federal government announced an emergency fisheries aid package, a restriction on the granting of new licences, and a ban on fishing for ground fish for some holders of part-time licences (Schrank et al., 1992, 352). Further declines in the catch of northern cod in 1990 and 1991 and a report by the Canadian Atlantic Fisheries Scientific Advisory Committee expressing concern about the paucity of adult fish resulted in quota reductions, and the establishment of a Task Force on Incomes and Adjustment in the Atlantic Fishery. Shortly after it reported, a total ban on commercial cod fishing was announced. The economy of the northeast coast of Newfoundland, which relies on those cod stocks that showed the most drastic decline in size, was especially affected.

The reasons for the stock decline have been subject to controversy. Factors assumed to be important include the actions of the Canadian offshore trawler fleet (destroying habitat, interrupting spawning, excessive dumping and discarding), overfishing and the use of undersize mesh by the foreign fleet off the Nose and Tail of the Grand Banks (just beyond the two-hundred-mile limit of Canada's fishery jurisdiction), too many seals, shortage of prey species like capelin, environmental factors, and poor scientific information (e.g., Meltzer, 1994; Schrank et al., 1992).

Government Adjustment Policies in the Outports

The complete devastation of the northern cod stocks has resulted in an economic and social crisis that threatens the very existence of outport life and culture.[1] The moratorium on commercial fishing has closed down the major source of seasonal employment for those who live in fishing villages, and has thus also affected eligibility for unemployment insurance.

Given the attachment of most residents to the outports (described in chapter 1) and the grim national unemployment picture for those willing to uproot, many of the citizens of the Newfoundland outports found themselves locked into a situation of enforced idleness, completely dependent on new government assistance schemes.

The federal government acted quickly when it closed the commercial fishery in 1992, setting up programs to aid those affected. The Northern Cod Adjustment and Recovery Program (NCARP) was the most important. NCARP (called the 'package' or the 'moratorium' locally) was designed as an emergency temporary program (ending 15 May 1994) to supplement incomes of affected fishermen and fish plant workers until major decisions could be made about the fishery (Task Force on Incomes and Adjustment in the Atlantic Fishery, 1993, 46). The level of individual support provided in the initial adjustment programs was set to be comparable to what people earned over the past three years, including unemployment insurance, with the maximum weekly benefit of $406.00 available to those who agreed to take part in full-time retraining aimed at upgrading basic educational skills and training for both fishery-related and unrelated work. For long-time plant workers and trawler men between the ages of fifty and sixty-four, the Plant Workers Adjustment program provided early retirement benefits of up to 70 per cent of the amount of unemployment insurance they were entitled to when they were laid off, to age sixty-four. The Vessel Support Program provided reimbursement for fishermen for costs related to storage and maintenance of their vessels. Other programs provided financial support for economic diversification projects in communities dependent on the fishery (Government of Canada News Release, 23 April 1993).

For a period of time following the 1993 election of a Liberal federal government to replace the former Conservative one, there appeared to be no clear indication of post-moratorium policy as the government struggled to come to grips with the extent of the problem. However, in late 1993 the government indicated that they would honour an election promise 'not to abandon fishers and fish plant workers in their time of need' (Department of Fisheries and Oceans News Release, 20 December 1993). The Atlantic Groundfish Strategy (TAGS) of 1994 essentially extended the provisions of the earlier adjustment programs for as long as five years (*Globe and Mail,* 23 April 1994, A10), the minimal period of time viewed as necessary to rebuild the fish stocks.[2] There was a small reduction in the maximum weekly benefit allowed in the adjustment program. Another goal of the TAGS program was eventually to reduce fishing capacity in Newfoundland by 50 per cent. The TAGS program was still in effect at the time of this writing (early 1996).

Without the adjustment programs, the collapse of the fishery would have undoubtedly forced so large a migration as to result in a desertion of many outports. For fishers in particular, the likelihood of migration is particulary low because fishing offers the only real possibility of significant earnings and a life style based on self-employment and outdoor activity, and the only way for a lifetime of knowledge and skill, acquired informally, to pay off. This sentiment was relayed by a Fish Arm fisherman who, when asked whether he had considered moving away from the village, said that he had never even considered moving to the mainland or even a city in Newfoundland, but had thought about moving to a larger community on Northern Bay. In dismissing the idea, he quickly pointed out that it would take him 'ten or fifteen years to build up again what he already had in Fish Arm.'

The Immediate Impact of the Moratorium on Outport Life

In some ways, outport life in Main Harbour and Fish Arm has not been very much affected by the moratorium. Like unemployment insurance, the receipt of moratorium support is seen as another resource whose benefit is to be optimized. Fishery adjustment payments during the moratorium are not stigmatizing, in part because, as with unemployment insurance benefits, there are a large number of recipients, and they have been 'earned' through prior work-force participation. The fact of unemployment is seen as a social issue, not a result of individual pathology (cf. Mills, 1959).

Not surprisingly, the key local concerns shortly after the closure of the fishery and the announcement of the adjustment packages centred around who was eligible, and what level of compensation one could obtain. Given the intimate knowledge of others' affairs, invidious distinctions were frequently made. People questioned the fairness of the procedures. Thus, one fish plant worker who 'had never missed a day's work in nineteen years,' except when seriously ill, and who 'slaved' for the fish plant, lamented the fact that fishermen were being compensated by the government when they sold back their fishing licences (as much as $50,000 for a salmon licence), but fish plant workers only received 'the moratorium.' Instances in which people such as spouses of fishermen or family members of fish plant managers somehow became eligible for moratorium payments, despite marginal attachments to the fishery labour force,[3] and others where people had the misfortune of not being eligible in spite of long service in the fishery, were the subject of intense commentary. In general, however, these concerns were kept at the level of local gossip, in part because there was no formal machinery for anonymous reporting (as there is for illegal hunting or fishing) and because of general support for maximizing family income from government sources both individually and collectively.

For fish plant workers and fishermen, the adjustment program, whose payments are based on average incomes over the past few years,[4] has resulted in a stabilization of income, albeit at a modest level. This has allowed for the purchase of some consumer necessities which may have been put off when incomes were more unpredictable – most obviously, major items like snowmobiles, automobiles, and housing materials, particularly among the less well off residents. Again, however, it should be noted that in many cases, used and lower-quality items are purchased (except for snowmobiles), and the items selected generally have practical value for the family household. For example, a few Fish Arm residents have bought used cars and trucks, often more than ten years old, in some cases parking them in Main Harbour. They are viable as modes of transportation only because local residents can repair and maintain them themselves. Overall, then, the moratorium has likely caused some levelling of income among fishermen, as all boats, including those of successful long-liner fishermen, have been tied up except for short periods when it is possible to fish for crab, capelin, and other non-traditional species.

The general orientation of outport residents who are recipients of moratorium benefits is to go along with the regulations of the programs. Some of the provisions of the fishery adjustment programs, like unemployment insurance provisions, mandate maintenance of local residency. Thus most outport residents, in spite of no longer having work commitments, remain in the local area, not being free to undertake longer trips that might interfere with their government incomes. Within the local area, however, the lack of work commitments has made possible a pattern of more extensive local visits to relatives and friends, more free time to pursue traditional outdoor leisure pursuits, and more frequent trips to larger centres, often for shopping or window shopping and social purposes (i.e., as an enjoyable outing with friends, not necessarily involving a purchase).

In terms of everyday activities, the most important feature of the fishery adjustment programs in the first couple of years has been the training component. This has involved courses for upgrading fishery-related skills on the one hand, and courses and training programs aimed at upgrading educational levels and retraining for new careers on the other. Both are being funded through the federal Department of Human Resources. People dutifully attend because higher moratorium payments are contingent upon attendance, but sense an underlying futility in taking courses that are perceived as unlikely to benefit them personally in the outport context. Some such courses are ridiculed, in the typical outport manner. After talking about some of his horrible experiences in elementary school, which had fortunately been cut short when he was forced to go fishing with his father, one informant expressed considerable concern about having to attend school after all these years, but shrugged it off by saying with a humorous grin, 'My son, after I finish, I'll be able to write a book!' Another example of the indirect questioning of the appropriateness of a training program occurred in regard to a course on self-esteem that was offered. The commentator observed that the course would have been a lot more valuable if it had been given when fishermen were getting only $100 per week, not when they were making $400.

Locally, in Fish Arm and Main Harbour, the fishing-related courses seem to be better accepted by those involved than the general retraining and educational upgrading courses. These fishing-related courses, however, are not exempt from being targets of humour. One person, for example, relayed an account of a first aid course he attended. The instructor was discussing what to do if someone got food stuck in his throat when there was no medical person around. A fisherman raised the question whether, if other attempts to dislodge the food failed, it was okay to use a knife to the neck to try to cut the food free. Before the instructor could answer, another course participant remarked that if he ever went in the woods with the fisherman who asked the question, the only thing he would take along to eat would be jelly! These local reactions expressing the perceived futility of many of the retraining programs appear to be general in Newfoundland (Task Force on Incomes and Adjustment in the Atlantic Fishery, 1993, 92). Another indication of this was the government plan to drop the requirement of entering a training program to receive moratorium payments (Department of Fisheries and Oceans News Release, 20 December 1993).

While there are drawbacks, the retraining component of the adjustment programs has had positive benefits for outport life. By keeping many otherwise idled adults busy, these courses may, in the short run, help 'fill in time' and prevent the demoralizing effects of having nothing to do. This in itself may help counter the frustration and hostility that sometimes ensue. In a few cases, it is conceivable that people will obtain sufficient training, skill, and motivation to pursue other careers either locally or outside of the community.[5] It is too early to determine the extent to which this will take place. A different approach that the adjustment programs have taken is to support the development of local entrepreneurship, in part through training programs.[6] This support is consonant with the 'small is beautiful' approach (Overton, 1990) of recent years, in which government policies are aimed at fostering self-reliance and encouraging small-scale business in order to reduce government dependency and help sustain life in the outports. These programs generally receive the support of outport residents. A number of tourist-oriented local enterprises have been started with government assistance and provide some employment locally, though so far most employment is part-time and necessitates government income supplementation.

The Effect of DFO's Recent Fishery Policy

In the wake of the collapse of the ground fish stocks, the Canadian government embarked on highly publicized international efforts to regulate the Atlantic fishery more closely. Since 1992, attempts to halt foreign overfishing have been central to this effort, and there has been some success. A media demonstration by Canadian fisheries minister Brian Tobin in New York City proving the use of undersize mesh by a foreign fishing boat brought the matter to worldwide attention. Given the low catches, the European Community has since agreed to abide by NAFO quotas and conservation decisions. In addition, fishing by non-NAFO boats, often flying flags of convenience, was halted; there was increased surveillance, and a dispute settlement mechanism was developed (Meltzer, 1994).

The collapse of the ground fish stocks also enabled the DFO to strengthen policy initiatives aimed at the inshore sector. These initiatives focus generally on reducing the number of inshore fishermen and more intensively regulating their activities. This section presents a brief description of the development of government policy and the enforcement strategies for the inshore fishery, followed by an analysis of the impact of these changes on social order and tension in the outports.

Intensive government regulation of the inshore fishery is a recent phenomenon. In the small-boat fishery (employing fixed gear such as hand lines and cod traps), which predominated until the mid-1970s, the fishermen basically policed themselves (Matthews and Phyne, 1988; A. Davis, 1991). Traditional co-operative arrangements included draws for fishing berths and restriction of certain gear types to certain locations, based on access to space. Matthews and Phyne (1988) describe the local regulation of the commons:

> Indeed, fishermen generally go out of their way to ensure that their activities do not infringe on the rights of others, and have even developed new regulations to protect those using older, less efficient technologies. It might be argued that such regulations are informal and can be easily broken at any time. However, such an argument does not take into account the taboolike quality such regulations have in the normative structure of these communities. To violate such regulations deliberately and knowingly might indeed lead to a battle in which they too can only lose. (168)

Importantly, Matthews and Phyne argue that traditional controls over the local fishery persist. The strength of these controls is suggested by events like the burning of DFO patrol boats that occurred in southwest Nova Scotia. This situation was caused in part by fishery officers engaging in practices that violated local norms regarding the handling of lobster pots (McMullan et al., 1988).[7]

The fishery crisis of the early 1970s (see chapter 2) marked a sea change in the regulation and enforcement of fishing policy for the Department of Fisheries and Oceans. The DFO adopted a Hobbesian view of the need for regulation. Stemming from a seminal article by Hardin (1968), the thrust of the new DFO philosophy, accepted by management and fishery officers alike, was the need to regulate sea resources to avoid a 'tragedy of the commons' that would inevitably occur if self-interested fishermen simply pursued their own economic ends (Matthews and Phyne, 1988). The earlier mode of compliance-based, reactive enforcement, whose goal was to avoid escalating the occasional conflict that occurred when informal social controls did not work, was replaced by a deterrence-based, proactive policy with an emphasis on enforcement. Fishery officers began to be trained with the RCMP and adopted more adversarial attitudes (Arai, 1994). The effectiveness of these changes, however, was limited by insufficient budgets, an inadequate number of personnel, and the difficulties of enforcing an increasingly complex myriad of regulations involving species-specific seasons, licences, fishing zones, size limits, and so on (McMullan et al., 1988; Arai, 1994).

Since the 1980s, a central plank in DFO efforts to conserve fish stocks has been to professionalize the fishery by reducing the number of fishermen. Categories of full-time and part-time licences were established to limit entry. The rights of part-time fishermen have been eroded. There have been periodic buy-outs so as to reduce the number dependent on the fishery.

These government policies have affected those with marginal attachments to the fishery the hardest. This group includes a large number of persons who work part-time in the fishery. There is a widening gap between those who are ultimately given licences to fish full time and those who are not, and concomitant indications of high levels of discontent amount the have-nots in Newfoundland's outports. Thus one part-time fisherman lamented the fact that he had made only $40 from May to August, and would have to sell his house and cabin, and was likely to lose his truck for non-payment of monthly instalments. He indicated resentment at the comment made by a neighbouring fisherman who said that the $53,000 he received from fishing for crab in one week 'was hardly worth the effort.'

The conflict of interest between full-time and part-time fishermen (and full-time fishermen whose licences do not enable them to make a reasonable living) has been made more explicit during the moratorium. For example, the Newfoundland Fishermen, Food and Allied Workers Union has supported efforts to save the fish for a smaller number of full-time professional fishermen. This sentiment was perhaps best expressed in the Cashin Report (the Task Force on Incomes and Adjustment in the Atlantic Fishery, 1993, was chaired by Richard Cashin, founder and leader of the NFFAW), which advocated the elimination of part-timers from the fishery and of any other policy that would enable part-time fishermen and others marginally attached to the fishery to retain a toehold.

What form of expression will the frustration of the disenfranchised take? It is unlikely that the informal but effective outport social control mechanisms described throughout this book will weaken so much that there will be an ominous increase in local crime, either personal or property. Indeed, the tendency of the community to 'pull together' in periods of hardship or in the face of threats to its existence may make interpersonal expression of frustration even more unlikely,[8] even among those most severely affected. Inasmuch as the worst-off segment, part-time fishers and plant workers, have few, if any, organized political channels or opportunities for expressing their sentiments and frustration beyond the community, the likely mode of adaptation to their grievances and frustrations will be civil disobedience and resistance to government policies and their enforcement, similar to that which has occurred in a tightly knit southwestern Nova Scotian fishing community whose citizens felt harassed by government officials (Grady and Sacouman, 1990). The 1994 harbour blockade by fishermen from a Cape Breton fishing village, incensed by what they saw as unfair government licensing policies that enriched some fishers while others made little or nothing, is another example. More recently, groups of disgruntled fisherman have occupied DFO offices in Nova Scotia and demonstrated against government policy in British Columbia.

There is a vicious circle at work in the relationship between government regulation, economic stratification, and discontent among fishermen. The decimation of the ground fish stocks has had a snowball effect on government regulation. Unable to fish for salmon, cod, and other main species, fishermen are putting more effort into other species that until recently have not been fished much. The crab fishery is a good example. The significant success of the few full-time crab fishermen resulted in demands from other fishermen for licences that would enable them to take part. However, the increased overall catches that resulted caused a drastic reduction in crab landings locally. This, in turn, laid the groundwork for further government regulation and enforcement, and the search for another source of fishery earnings.

The Criminalization of Subsistence Activities

The commercial fishery of the northeast coast of Newfoundland is particularly dependent on ground fish stocks. The complete closure of the *commercial* cod fishery in the area has been accompanied by sharp reductions in the total allowable catches of other ground fish stocks and a host of other conservation measures to reduce the catch of small fish and lessen fishing effort (Department of Fisheries and Oceans News Release, 20 December 1993). The goal of all of these efforts has been to rebuild fish stocks. Until January of 1994, the restrictions on cod fishing did not extend to fishing for personal consumption (mislabelled by the DFO as the 'recreational' fishery). Indeed, the ability to feed one's family from local sea resources has been a traditional practice and perceived right and necessity among impoverished fishermen for as long as Newfoundland outports have existed.

Upon advice from the Fisheries Resource Conservation Council that as much as ten thousand tonnes of codfish was caught in the recreational fishery over the past two years,[9] and lobbied by the major fishing union, the Newfoundland Fishermen, Food and Allied Workers Union, early in 1994, the federal government closed the recreational cod fishery across the province (*Globe and Mail*, 1 February 1994). To enforce this closure, penalties were set that included the possibility of having all gear and vehicles seized, fines of up to $100,000, and sentences of up to a year in jail. To enforce these provisions, new management measures for the recreational fishery were to be established in some regions of Atlantic Canada.

The concern for conservation brought about by the moratorium has also accelerated the regulation and restriction of other foraging activities, a trend that was underway prior to 1992. Motivated by threats to fishing incomes from a failing fishery, and by values of independence and self-reliance and a way of life that involves occupational pluralism and foraging, outport citizens have continued to engage in domestic economic activities in order to supplement their cash incomes from government assistance. As in the commercial fishery, where this involves the exploitation of local, renewable natural resources, the collective result is often over-exploitation beyond the ability of the resource to renew itself, and either a collapse of the resource, or regulation by the government, both of which have the same effect: closing another avenue of outport subsistence. The pattern is exacerbated by the effectiveness of communication channels in the outports. The success of one or a few is some endeavour is quickly made public and others soon follow suit. What provides a good livelihood for a few may be destroyed by many. The recent closure of the recreational cod and salmon fishery in the outports has resulted in a search for other ways of supplementing income. Cutting of firewood for others is a good example. In Main Harbour, residents (especially older ones) will purchase a pickup truck-load of firewood from a local individual, who typically prefers to cut logs as close to the 'highroad' as possible so as to make it more convenient and less expensive to haul them out. The net result has been an increasing number of ugly clear-cut areas close to the roads and the decimation of local stands of birch, a hardwood that burns longer and cleaner than the black spruce and other softwood species that abound in the area. This, in turn, has resulted in the possibility that cutting will be regulated, as occurred in a neighbouring community, and the necessity of going further into the woods to find firewood.

The 'tragedy of the commons' scenario has dramatically changed life in the outports. Where two decades ago there was very little effective external regulation of traditional outport economic activities, there is now increasing regulation, intensive enforcement, and severe punishment for violators, in the name of resource conservation. Much of the economic activity that provided the basis of the traditional outport way of life has been outlawed.

The Enforcement of Conservation Policy

The enforcement of hunting regulations was described in depth in chapter 4. This section describes the enforcement of fishing regulations during the moratorium and community reactions to the enforcement. Because of the shut-down of the cod and salmon fishery which forms the backbone of the commercial sector in this region, fishery enforcement efforts have focused primarily on policing the recreational fishery. These efforts, then, are directed squarely against traditional outport activities.

With the commercial fishing boats largely idle, it appears to some outport residents that fishery officers have little else to do than watch local citizens and make sure they are not involved in jigging a cod or netting a salmon or fishing trout without a licence. On one recent occasion, for example, a group of several local adults, two out-of-province guests, and a number of children set out by automobile along a dirt road to a secluded spot about forty-five minutes' drive from Main Harbour. They wanted to fish for trout, have a picnic, and generally enjoy the outdoors, a customary pursuit in the region. Within half an hour of their arrival, a local fishery officer, who had noted their departure from Main Harbour and who was known to all, arrived and check for trout licences, which were required for out-of-province guests. That such activity was increasingly common was express by a Main Harbour woman, who, upon hearing of the incident, stated, 'No wonder there's no fish. The brass buttons are blinding them.'

On another occasion, a group left Fish Arm for a pleasure cruise and shore lunch at a deserted settlement about two hours' steam away, by long liner. They did not observe any other boat in the waters on their journey. Arriving at their destination, which was a cove from which one could not see the open waters of Northern Bay, the captain had difficulty securing the grapple (a homemade anchor) on the sea bottom. On one attempt to do so, the grapple got caught on an old gill net, forcing all three adult males on board to work together to haul it out of the water. While they were hauling in the net, a large Coast Guard boat suddenly appeared in the cove. Quickly the captain issued instructions to turn the long liner around so that the cabin of the boat would block the view of the men working to untangle the net from the anchor. The net was allowed to fall back into the sea unnoticed by anyone from the Coast Guard boat. As the captain suspected, there were fishery officers on board the Coast Guard boat, and their purpose in entering the cove was to check out fishing violations. Recounting the event later, the captain said he was really concerned that if he had been caught with the gill net on board, he would have been liable for a large fine. He also indicated that the new federal government policy of fishery officers using Coast Guard boats to enforce regulations had changed fishermen's perceptions of the Coast Guard. Fishermen used to be happy to see a Coast Guard boat. The Coast Guard (whose duties include sea rescues and the maintenance of sea markers, etc.) used to be seen as the 'fishermen's friend,' but, with their new duties as escorts for fishery officers, this was no longer the case. A Coast Guard boat now spells potential trouble for the fishermen.

The end result of the intensive and heavy-handed enforcement effort aimed, perhaps by default, at the recreational fishery has been a feeling of harassment and victimization among many outport residents. This has been exacerbated by the imposition of severe penalties for fishing for purposes of family consumption, something that has always been done in the outports and that usually involves small quantities of fish. Community reactions are indicated in the following incident, which was described by two separate informants. Two young men in a boat were checking a salmon net that someone else had set, illegally. They were photographed by a fishery officer hiding on the shore. Despite their not have taken a salmon or set the net, their boat and motor, worth about $9000, were seized and they were fined $1500 each. Both observers indicated that the penalties were exceedingly harsh, given the low income of these individuals and the fact that they hadn't 'touched a scale.'

The sense of victimization has been heightened by local knowledge that trawlers working in Newfoundland waters are known to have dumped thousands of pounds of cod and other species and received relatively small fines, when caught,[10] and by the unregulated harvesting, only recently halted, of cod by foreign fishing boats off the Nose and Tail of the Grand Banks.

The criminalization of subsistence fishing has had another deleterious effect on outport life. Reporting of violations of the new regulations has become, in some cases, a means of social revenge. The situation is almost identical to the problem created by anonymous poacher hot lines discussed in chapter 4. Fishery officers are usually local residents who are known to act on tips of illicit activity, which can be given anonymously over the phone. Anonymous informants can report criminalized activity without incurring the sanctions associated with getting others in trouble that the visibility of behaviour in the outports would otherwise entail. A Fish Arm case will illustrate this. A former resident, on one of his frequent trips back to the village with an acquaintance, was given a couple of salmon as a gift by another resident to take back home, a common practice prior to the recent ban on salmon fishing and possession. They left by boat and arrived at Main Harbour, where they had parked their truck, and proceeded to hitch the boat to it. On the way out of Main Harbour, they were stopped in a roadblock and were charged by a local fishery officer with illegal possession of salmon. This incident resulted in seizure of the truck, boat, and salmon and an as yet undetermined court disposition. The reported reaction of the resident was outrage that, after all he had done for residents of Fish Arm, someone had got him into trouble. He reputedly said at the time that it would be 'a long time before he returned to Fish Arm.' One inadvertent result of the criminalization of community-supported traditional behaviour, then, is an increase in interpersonal suspicion among community residents and a breakdown of community solidarity.

The development and enforcement of the new conservation policies in regard to fishing and hunting, and the severe penalties for those caught, have greatly diminished the ability of outport residents to remain self-sufficient through traditional domestic production and have undermined the mutual sharing and co-operation that provided a buffer for many through hard times in the past. Unable to fish commercially or eke out a subsistence through traditional means, and unlikely to find a job elsewhere in Canada that will improve their lives, many of the citizens of the Newfoundland outports now find themselves idle and completely dependent on government assistance schemes. In view of the federal and provincial government deficits, it is fortunate that government adjustment programs have allowed most outport residents affected by the moratorium to maintain the status quo in terms of cash income. The level of benefits, however, is relatively low because of low fish plant wages and fish prices, a situation which is itself made possible by the fact that outport residents have been able to supplement their wage income with domestic production. The new prohibitions on hunting and fishing for family consumption mean that outport residents will now have to buy, at outport prices, which are generally higher than prices in urban areas, foodstuffs that they previously obtained through their own efforts or through kinship and friendship networks.

Likely Outport Responses during the New 'Hard Times'

Will the current state of affairs in the outports result in increased criminal activity, and if so, what type? The major government commission report (Task Force on Incomes and Adjustment in the Atlantic Fishery, 1993) documented the dimensions of the economic catastrophe that has hit Newfoundland, but generally had little to say about the behavioural consequences of the economic and social dilemma caused by the moratorium.

The theme of this book has been that patterns of crime and social order need to be understood in relation to the culture of the outports that has developed over the past centuries and remains, by and large, intact. People in the outports of Newfoundland still live in small, close-knit, isolated villages among kin and friends and are supportive of the outport life style. Under these conditions, the informal social control processes that have served to reduce and channel interpersonal hostility and crime still operate effectively. The intimacy of the outports means that individual problems as well as predicaments that are of concern to the community as a whole are likely to be incessantly discussed among family, other relatives, friends, informal groupings, and so on.

If history is a guide, collective action will be the outport way for expressing frustration with unpopular policies and decisions made from afar that are perceived to harm local citizens. Among disenfranchised and powerless outport residents, rows and riots have in the past regularly attended unpopular court cases and parliamentary legislation.

At present, the federal government's compensation of those directly affected by the moratorium has held in check the direct, collective expression of frustration caused by economic uncertainty, forced idleness, and policies that outlaw traditional and necessary economic practices. A shift in this precarious balance, perhaps triggered by a lessening of direct economic support from adjustment programs or by a more rigid enforcement of policies outlawing subsistence economic behaviour, is likely to tip the balance and result in the collective expression of outrage by those most directly affected and with the least to lose. Their likely target will be officials locally charged with enforcing policies developed and passed elsewhere.

Towards Enlightened Policy

The argument of the last section is based on the assumption that economic pressures will underlie potential collective responses in the outports directed against government intervention and enforcement. It follows that the prevention of moratorium-induced crime will also entail economic policy, since the culture of the outports is essentially non-violent. No one in Atlantic Canada doubts the need for massive improvements in policies with the goal of better conservation of fish stocks and sustainable yields. With the foreign fishing interests under control, it is clear that future choices about commercial fishing (if and when the stocks rebuild) will revolve around the apportionment of the overall catch between the offshore and inshore sectors, and among individuals or corporate entities within these sectors. Most debate has centred around the between-sector apportionment. The extreme positions are exemplified at one end by Schrank et al. (1992), who call for the allocation of fish stocks on the basis of efficiency and therefore favour the offshore sector, and at the other by Sinclair (1990), who advocates favouring the small-boat inshore sector on the grounds of social justice and resource conservation. It is clear that difficult decisions will need to be taken if the Atlantic fishery revives.

Government policy concerning how to apportion the catch among persons and boats within the inshore sector is as yet unclear. There is certainly an avowed general goal to reduce the number of inshore fishermen. The over-zealous enforcement of recreational fishery regulations and steep fines and penalties for violators, which are out of line with their impact on the fish stocks, suggest that the federal government is employing a conservation ideology to pursue policies whose purpose is ultimately to reduce transfer payments and government supports by weeding out the marginally employed. It is unable to do this directly, since severe cutbacks in the adjustment programs would be political suicide in the province of Newfoundland.

Instead of engaging in practices which make criminal the outport way of life, government policy should take advantage of the admirable outport values of resourcefulness, hard work, and self-sufficiency. The outport orientation is to take advantage of whatever resources are locally available in order to forge a living. In the short term, given the residents' relatively small numbers, the current trend to having small families, and their dispersion in small, isolated communities, it does not make sense, even from a conservation perspective, to regulate, enforce, and punish so heavily *subsistence* activities such as hunting, fishing, or cutting trees. Outport citizens have always sanctioned those who abused resources (such as killing game without consuming it). Government policy should be aimed at educating, providing guidelines for the use of renewable resources, and supplementing informal use norms that have developed over time. These traditional activities remain economically important and, what is more significant, culturally and psychologically fulfilling. Continued engagement in domestic production provides culturally meaningful activity and work and will help prevent the decline of the outports of Newfoundland into the demoralization and despondency characteristic of urban welfare ghettoes.

In the longer term, particularly for younger persons in the outports, enlightened government policies should tap into these same outport values. Certainly, more can be made of the remaining sea resources. The seas off of Newfoundland are still probably the world's richest fishing grounds. There are already some attempts to utilize different species and to use methods of fishing which result in sustainable catches, such as diving for scallops. Once shown that a process or method works, outport citizens are quick to catch on and copy it.

Particularly for fishermen, putting in long hours of hard work is not a problem. The orientation among fishermen is strongly individual, so innovations that can be handled by one person or by a small crew or work group will be most readily accepted. Less than a year after the first long liner was brought into Fish Arm, for example, several people had built their own from local materials. Thus, in fishing, innovations such as improved refrigeration systems on long liners, freezing fish at sea, as is done with salmon on Canada's west coast, and the use of line-and-hook as opposed to netting techniques would be most quickly adopted. It would only take a few successful experiments on the Island of Newfoundland to spread a new technique among fishermen. In the fish processing sector, more local processing instead of exporting minimally processed raw sea food (such as squid) would keep jobs at home.

Government attempts to retrain younger workers affected by the moratorium are laudable. Amongst this quintessentially practical and locally oriented population, those programs that result in saleable skills and have visible occupational benefits will be more successful than those that involve general educational upgrading or less applied skills. Again, what is needed are a few successful role models. Government should also place more emphasis on the great opportunity for higher education and specialized training that is now possible because of the fishery adjustment programs and emphasize that it is a once-in-a-lifetime chance for people who previously could not afford the time or money to attend courses. Though it is likely that those who find better opportunities elsewhere will leave, it should also be made clear that acceptance of funding for training does not *necessitate* leaving the outports.

Notes

1: Introduction

1 This title is taken from a series of tourist-oriented television commercials aimed at attracting visitors to Newfoundland and Labrador.

2 This is not to say that all or even most urban crime is committed by strangers. Indeed, some types of urban crime are generally committed by people known to each other.

3 See Brym and Sacouman (1979) for an interesting discussion of the terms used by political economists to describe the status of fishermen in relation to the wider economy.

4 There is a large differentiation by gender in the economic activities of men and women in the outports.

5 Concessions by the government of Newfoundland have resulted in large tracts of timber rights now being possessed by two large companies.

6 Cabot Martin (1990, 268) has described this period as the social scientific conquest of his province: 'formidable phalanxes of anthropologists and folklorists descended on us like gold prospectors, enthusing over the vast, untapped resource that was Newfoundland's cultural history.'

7 In its strictest use, 'rough food,' the title of Omohundro's book, referred to 'your staples, your winter's diet ... the things you got in the fall to see you through 'til spring,' according to one of Omohundro's informants (1993, xiii). More generally, the term is 'emblematic of the traditional lifestyle which depended heavily on self sufficiency to supplement a small and unreliable income from fishing and logging' (xiv).

8 Felt et al. (1995b, 101) argue that some activities, such as moose hunting, are undertaken for cultural as well as economic reasons, as they are engaged in by individuals who could easily purchase substitutes. The fact

that outport residents continue to engage in pluralistic, foraging activities supports the view that much of the outport culture described in the classic era remains intact today.

9 A resident of one of the research sites estimated that it would take about a thousand sticks (local trees cut and limbed) to build a house. The work would involve a few weeks' work cutting the trees with a chain-saw, waiting until winter to drag them by snowmobile to a local sawmill, transporting the rough-cut lumber to his yard, and piling it for a year or so of natural drying. Finally, one could begin to build a house from the yield of lumber, buying whatever supplies were needed from a hardware store.

10 Successful merchants and fish buyers seem to take pains to hide their economic success from the community, as their profits come from dealings with the community itself and ostentation would likely engender more resentment.

11 See chapter 2 for some recent statistics on income, unemployment levels, occupational distributions, etc.

12 Chapter 10 notes that the current crisis in the fishery and subsequent government regulation of many traditional subsistence activities have recently threatened the ability of outport residents to provide for themselves.

13 One older woman, for example, calculated that she spent about three months' worth of old age pension cheques on Christmas gifts for practically all close and distant relatives.

14 This is the title of an article on return migration by Richling (1985).

15 Indeed, Felt and Sinclair (1995a, 13) indicate that it appears that many individuals, particularly young males, make an attempt to leave their community to find a job elsewhere, primarily to legitimate their place in the community upon returning ('at least I tried'). Their return also legitimates the decision of those who remained.

16 See chapter 3 for a more detailed description of the physical and environmental features of the particular villages along the northeast coast that were the research sites.

17 For example, Porter (1983) observed that younger women from Aquaforte, a fishing village close to St John's, aspired to attain an urban life style and were dissatisfied with the life of fisherman's wife.

2: A History of Outport Settlement, Economic Development, and Law Enforcement

1 Neis (1991) notes that technological advancements, which led to cheaper chicken production in the United States, and competition from Korean and Argentinian fish also lowered fish prices in Newfoundland.

2 To the tune of $100 million for both Fishery Products International and National Sea, the latter being an essentially Nova Scotia company (Schrank et al., 1987). An additional $281 million was poured into FPI from government sources between 1983 and 1985 (Schrank et al., 1992).

3 Cod was still the backbone of the seasonal inshore fishery, but a number of other species had become important sources of income, including squid, capelin, turbot, and other ground fish. These species made up 80 per cent of the province's landings (Newfoundland Department of Rural, Agricultural and Northern Development, 1983, 67; Task Force on Incomes and Adjustment in the Atlantic Fishery, 1993, 5).

4 In municipalities where the population is less than fifteen thousand, including the research sites for this study, Main Harbour and Fish Arm, the province paid 62 per cent of the total cost of the RCMP and the federal government 38 per cent, but the federal proportion was slated to decrease slowly over time.

5 The Newfoundland Constabulary's jurisdiction was expanded in the mid-1980s to include the northeast Avalon Peninsula and Labrador West, including Labrador City, Wabush, and Churchill Falls. In 1986, the second largest city in Newfoundland, Corner Brook, was added, leaving the RCMP comprising almost exactly half of the province's police strength.

6 Newfoundland has just under six hundred people per police officer in Canada, which, next to Prince Edward Island, is the highest ratio among provinces in Canada. However, the dispersed population usually means that the actual presence of police in a village is somewhat rare, unless the village also contains the detachment.

3: The Setting

1 In order to ensure confidentiality of information, all places associated with the research sites have been given fictitious names. In addition, all respondents have been identified by randomly selected letters only, and, where deemed necessary, some information which could serve to identify individuals has been changed to protect identities. For example, if a description of sensitive information involved twins, but the twin relation was immaterial to the description involved, the individuals involved might be termed 'relatives,' since calling them 'twins' would almost certainly enable them to be identified. To further ensure confidentiality, references to places in the bibliography have been changed to 'a Northeast Coast Community.'

2 One family of brothers and their wives and children have settled in a cove known for its lucrative salmon fishing, but they are not considered to 'belong' to either community studied.

3 One older Main Harbour woman, who was taken on an automobile drive along the scenic Cabot Trail in Cape Breton, Nova Scotia, complained that she could see all the trees and hills she wanted (back) home.

4 In describing the reason he settled in the Main Harbour area, one professional from the United States said he studied climatological maps and chose the area because it has a large number of sunny days.

5 This estimate is the average of the 750 figure for the early 1980s and the 650 figure obtained for 1994. The earlier figures were based on a survey conducted by the Anglican minister. The same figure of 750 was obtained independently from the provincial court judge of the jurisdiction, for 1986.

6 The coast of Newfoundland where the French held fishing and curing rights until 1904 (Story et al., 1982, 202).

7 A pejorative term for a person of mixed Indian and French ancestry, more commonly found on the west coast of Newfoundland.

8 There is some confusion about the actual settlement dates by anglophones, as the government of Newfoundland and Labrador Census of 1884 put the local population at fifty-two, and other sources go back as far as 1857. It is worth keeping in mind that most outport fishing settlements were located within easy rowing distance of good fishing berths, most of which allowed only a few families to wrest a living from the sea.

9 This road was paved during the middle of the research period.

10 See Sparkes (1983) for an autobiographical account of life in a self-sufficient community with agricultural resources similar to Main Harbour, and a polemic on the loss of autonomy through reliance on merchants and the government for subsistence.

11 This is indicated by the lack of local names differentiating the sections.

12 Personal communication with the minister.

13 These are primarily older models whose bodies are in various states of disrepair, though they have been kept running mechanically. Most are not licensed, since they only travel up and down the same road.

14 Typically, a British-trained nurse served the community in the past, but the most recent nurse is a Newfoundland native from another community.

4: Crime Rates and Crime Reporting in the Outports

1 Official rates of violent crime in Newfoundland, while lower than the Canadian average, are generally higher than in Prince Edward Island and New Brunswick.

2 Laub's definition of 'rural' included all areas outside of Standard Metropolitan Statistical Areas, a category which includes areas from those with

very sparse populations all the way to cities with a population of up to fifty thousand. Since the outports examined in this study had populations of less than one thousand, it is unclear how relevant Laub's study is.

3 Though this information was collected a few years before the field work began, it is the only available breakdown of local crime known to me. The information was derived from a report by a private consulting firm that was hired to assess the prospects and potential problems of constructing a large natural resource project close to one of the research sites. One of the residents of the community made it available.

4 Gunness (1973, 123) reports an incident similar to this one, supporting the idea of widespread fear of police in the outports.

5: Patterns of Outport Big Game Poaching

1 The inclusion of fishermen is the result of papers sent to Brymer by the author (see Brymer, 1990, 13).

2 McGrath (1992, 16) reports that in the late 1980s, opposition to the growth of outdoor tourism by groups fearful of losing traditional use and access rights forced the government to withdraw proposed legislation.

3 Brymer (1990, 15–16) notes that in Ontario and many other jurisdictions, game wardens operate under a broader legal mandate than the usual police authorities, particularly in terms of powers of search without a warrant.

4 Despite the war on poaching that was declared in the early 1980s, the climate of fiscal restraint in that period resulted in budget cutbacks; as a result, the number of wildlife officers decreased, as did funding for support equipment. Officers had to make do with existing equipment (McGrath, 1992, 16).

5 A shareman is a fisherman who works on a boat owned by someone else and who is paid on the basis of a set share, or portion of the catch.

6 Even allowing for a certain amount of exaggeration, it is undoubtedly true that this person's food costs were lowered considerably through hunting and trapping.

7 Firestone (1978, 103), in his study of the northeast coast outport of Savage Cove, indicated that competition among men occurred over anything and everything, but particularly catches of fish, seals, and hares.

6: The Modus Operandi of the Poacher: A Case Study

1 In wooded areas where snowmobiles cannot ride two or more abreast,

single file is the only way to ride, and the person in the lead is usually one who knows the way to the destination or is least likely to get lost. If the snow is deep, the leader must also 'break the trail,' which is physically more demanding than following others' snowmobiles tracks. Sometimes men take turns breaking the trail. If, for some reason, those who are following cannot keep up with the others, they rely on those in the lead to note that they are 'missing.' This is especially important when riders get spread out while travelling fast. The practice is for those who note that others are missing to allow a considerable amount of time for them to catch up, on the assumption that they were delayed by some small inconvenience. To turn back right away would signal lack of confidence in the individual's ability to fix whatever problem delayed him and would be taken as something of an insult. A longer delay signals that something major is wrong and one should circle back, given the danger of a breakdown or injury in the woods kilometres away from service stations, mechanics or medical care.

2 A large animal like this one provides about 150–200 pounds per quarter and forms an important protein source for the families and friends with whom it will be shared.

7: Moonshine

1 A retail outlet for the Board of Liquor Control (cf. Story et al., 1982, 113).

2 High school students from Fish Arm and Main Harbour attend school at an outport about twenty miles from Main Harbour. This entails boarding out for Fish Arm residents, but students return home by ferry almost every weekend when possible. Main Harbour students are bused to and from high school.

3 Persons under age nineteen are not allowed to purchase alcohol in Newfoundland.

4 The commercial ground fish moratorium initiated in 1992 has certainly created more free time for many outport residents whose jobs rely on the fishery. However, the establishment of important fisheries for non-traditional species, notably capelin and crab, has kept many fishermen busy, though not as busy as in the past. One fisherman remarked upon walking from one end of Fish Arm to the other that 'this is the first time I've done this since I was a teenager.'

5 There were only a few bachelors around, and I did not have close research contact with them. Single men living in their own residences undoubtedly have the opportunity to make moonshine, but at the same time are likely

to have sufficient surplus cash to make the purchase of beer possible. Single adult males living with relatives or boarding out likely do not have access to facilities for making moonshine in privacy.

6 A conversation with a teacher at the local high school revealed that, judging from student talk after weekends, some students were making as well as drinking moonshine.

7 The liquor content of a gallon of 150-proof moonshine is approximately equal to two gallons of store-bought liquor, or about three forty-ounce bottles, which would cost about $90.00. Assuming that a 1½-ounce drink would be the equivalent of a bottle of beer, a gallon of moonshine would be the equivalent of about seven dozen beers, which in Newfoundland would cost more than $100. One informant indicated that the cost of materials for producing a forty-ounce bottle of moonshine in the early 1980s when he was 'at it all the time' was about $1.50. It is still very low today, compared to liquor purchased from the government liquor outlets. The cost of liquor and beer is higher in Newfoundland than other provinces.

8: Interpersonal Crime and Vandalism

1 This is not to say that the victim just forgot about it. Years later, he still remembered the incident, with some bitterness.

2 This abstention was clearly not absolute, as I had on several occasions shared beer with UT. Thus, quitting drinking may refer to heavy drinking.

3 Pushing, grabbing, shoving, and slapping were classed as 'minor violence,' and kicking, hitting, beating up, and threatening with a knife or gun were classed as 'severe violence' in Kennedy and Dutton's (1989) survey of domestic violence in Alberta. Canadian and American survey data indicate that about one in five men commits an act of violence against his spouse in a year, and one in ten commits an act of severe violence against his spouse in a lifetime.

4 At the time of the research, this television program was 'All My Children.'

5 The *Dictionary of Newfoundland English* defines a 'hard ticket' as 'anyone who is constantly getting into trouble, fighting frequently or playing practical jokes' (Story et al., 1990, 241). This usage of the term emphasizes the non-fighting aspect of the label.

6 A visitor from a different outport said that people like the repeat offenders described above would be 'run out of town' where he came from.

7 During an interview, the local judge serving the Main Harbour area described the typical offender as an eighteen- or nineteen-year-old male

involved in a liquor-related offence. He attributed much of the crime to high levels of unemployment, the lack of organized activities or anything to do, and subsequent drinking of alcohol (field notes, Judge O).

8 Tonnies' description of *gemeinschaft* seems to fit here. Indeed, other social scientists have variously referred to outport life as feudal society, peasant society, and so on (Szwed, 1966). In this section, however, I am referring specifically to the nature of social interaction rather than an economic dimension.

9: Crimes of the Powerful

1 The 1994 revelations of illicit homosexual acts carried out with impunity at the Mount Cashel Orphanage in Newfoundland will probably not surprise observers of outport life.

2 One successful Fish Arm fisherman indicated that, as a result of poor catches in the previous year, he planned to follow a school of fish as they moved along the coast of Newfoundland, selling the catch to different plants along the way. He did not implement this plan, however, because of the imposition of the commercial fishing moratorium in 1992.

3 Palmer (1995a) indicates that fishermen prefer to sell their catch to their local community fish plant in order to maintain employment for local individuals, often including kin and friends.

4 Retail store prices in the Atlantic provinces generally do not make this distinction when selling to the public.

5 Fish buyers and plant operators, of course, have their own pressures to deal with. The prices they charge are determined not only by an interest in keeping the monies paid to fishermen low, but also by world market prices.

6 Sider (1986, 29) notes that the credit arrangements with the merchants were made to ensure that fisher families continually needed credit to get access to the sea.

7 In 1994, the period of eligibility was increased to twelve weeks.

8 See Sider (1986) for a description of the historic necessity of unending labour at fish-related and other economic activities which underlay the development of the value of hard work. Chapter 8 also discusses the value of competitiveness in the outports.

9 A short-lived town council was eventually disbanded prior to the research period. Its main business seemed to be the disposal of garbage, a problem that is still unresolved.

10 It should be noted that the perception of some in the community was that the successful applicant was, of all the people in the outport, the best

suited to get the grant, given his resources and experience. Since holders of this belief would be unlikely to apply for such grants, this would constitute a self-fulfilling prophecy.

11 In one case, an informant said that the wife of a dominant merchant asked a pre-teen girl who happened to be passing the house to come inside and sweep the floor. Being exceptionally independent, the girl told her saucily that she was no servant and to sweep the floor herself. The girl's mother, however, upon hearing of the refusal, became quite concerned and castigated the girl.

10: Government Policy and Social Order in a Collapsed Economy

1 The magnitude of the economic devastation is documented in the report of the Task Force on Incomes and Adjustment in the Atlantic Fishery (1993, chapter 9).

2 *Maclean's* magazine (23 August 1993) pegged the cost of TAGS at $800 million per year.

3 In response to a report by the federal auditor-general criticizing payment of some $15 million out of the $587 million Northern Cod Adjustment and Recovery Program, a former federal fisheries minister, John Crosbie, defended the program by arguing that it had to be designed quickly because 'Newfoundland fishermen would have gone hungry' waiting for a better program (Halifax *Mail-Star*, 22 January 1994, D22).

4 The average compensation was $282 per week (*Globe and Mail*, 23 April 1994, A10), for a yearly income of $14,664. This is about two-thirds of the average income of all individuals in Newfoundland in 1990, which was $21,600 (Task Force on Incomes and Adjustment in the Atlantic Fishery, 1993, table 18–2, 163).

5 For example, one Fish Arm woman recently received a grant to teach idled workers sewing skills that might be used to expand a cottage industry of making customized cold weather clothing.

6 Some of these programs predate the collapse of the fishery.

7 See also Palmer (1995a) for a description of co-operative arrangements worked out so that dragger fishermen could operate up and down the Straits of Belle Isle. Local fishermen allowed it, knowing that the next year they might have to do the same.

8 A recent disappearance of a fisherman from Fish Harbour indicates the continued strength of community norms. For two weeks after the disappearance, fishermen combed the area searching for the body, which was never found. This was done at great personal expense, both in terms of the

cost of keeping boats going, and in terms of foregone fishing income during the height of the fishing season. No one wanted to be the first to give up. The search ended only when the fisherman's wife made a public request.

9 A local fisherman indicated that there may have been a problem with abuse of 'recreational' fishing rights along the south coast of Newfoundland, with people selling fish rather than using it for their own consumption, but there was no such abuse, as far as he knew, in Northern Bay.

10 For example, in 1994 two National Sea Products offshore trawler captains who illegally dumped twenty-two thousand pounds of cod while fishing for redfish in the Gulf of St Lawrence off of Newfoundland's southwest coast were fined $15,000 and $20,000 each (Halifax *Mail-Star*, 5 May 1994, A15).

Bibliography

Alexander, David. 1980. 'Newfoundland's Traditional Economy and Development to 1934.' In J.K. Hiller and Peter Neary, eds. *Newfoundland in the Nineteenth and Twentieth Centuries: Essays in Interpretation.* Toronto: University of Toronto Press. 17–39.

Ames, Randy. 1977. 'Socio-Economic and Legal Problems of Hunting in Northern Labrador.' Nain, Labrador: Commissioned by the Labrador Inuit Association.

Andersen, Raoul. 1972. 'Hunt and Deceive: Information Management in Newfoundland Deep-Sea Trawler Fishing.' In R. Andersen and C. Wadel, eds. *North Atlantic Fishermen: Anthropological Essays on Modern Fishing.* St John's: Institute of Social and Economic Research, Memorial University of Newfoundland.

Andrews, Peter, and Jocelyn D. Wells. 1973. "The Making of Moonshine, Homebrew, Wines, Brandies, and Other Homemade Beverages in Nfld.' Undergraduate paper submitted to Folklore 3400. Memorial University of Newfoundland Folklore and Language Archive, accession no. 73–105.

Antler, Ellen. 1977. 'Women's Work in Newfoundland Fishery Families.' *Atlantis: A Women's Studies Journal* 2. 106–13.

Arai, A. Bruce. 1994. 'Policy and Practice in the Atlantic Fisheries: Problems of Regulatory Enforcement.' *Canadian Public Policy* 20:4. 353–64.

Brazil, Terry. 1979. 'Northeast Coast Community Moonshine.' Undergraduate paper submitted to Folklore 2000. Memorial University of Newfoundland Folklore and Language Archive, accession no. 79–464.

Brown, Linda. 1975. 'Christmas Customs in a Northeast Coast Community.' Undergraduate paper submitted to Folklore 3420. Memorial University of Newfoundland Folklore and Language Archive, accession no. 75–10.

Brox, Ottar. 1972. *Newfoundland Fishermen in the Age of Industry: A Sociology of*

Dualism. Newfoundland Social and Economic Studies no. 9. St John's: Institute of Social and Economic Research, Memorial University of Newfoundland.

Brym, R.J., and R.J. Sacouman. 1979. *Underdevelopment and Social Movements in Atlantic Canada*. Toronto: New Hogtown Press.

Brymer, Richard A. 1990. 'The Emergence and Maintenance of a Deviant Sub-Culture: The Case of Hunting/Poaching Subculture.' 29 May 1990 unpublished version. Department of Sociology, McMaster University, Hamilton, Ontario.

Chambers, Marie. 1974. 'Dynamics of Interaction and the Moral Order of a Small Community: Past, Present and Future.' Paper submitted to Sociology 2230 (Professor T. Nemec). Memorial University of Newfoundland.

Chambliss, William J., and Robert B. Seidman. 1971. *Law, Order and Power*. Reading, Mass.: Addison-Wesley.

Charles, Anthony T. 1992. 'Fishery Conflicts: A Unified Framework.' *Marine Policy* 16:2. 379–93.

Chiaramonte, Louis J. 1979. 'Christmas in Deep Harbour: Aspects of Social Organization in Mumming and Drinking.' Unpublished paper in Centre for Newfoundland Studies, Memorial University of Newfoundland. St John's: Department of Sociology and Anthropology, Memorial University of Newfoundland.

Copes, Parzival. 1972. *The Resettlement of Fishing Communities in Newfoundland*. Ottawa: Canadian Council on Rural Development.

Courtis, Malcolm, and I. Dessuyer. 1970. *Attitudes to Crime and the Police in Toronto: A Report on Some Survey Findings*. Toronto: Centre of Criminology, University of Toronto.

Crane, Norman. 1982. 'The Newfoundland Rangers.' Paper delivered to the Newfoundland Historical Society. In Centre for Newfoundland Studies, Memorial University of Newfoundland.

Davis, Dona Lee. 1979. 'Social Structure, Sex Roles and Female Associations in a Newfoundland Fishing Village.' Unpublished paper. Centre for Newfoundland Studies, Memorial University of Newfoundland.

– 1988. '"Shore Skippers and Grass Widows": Active and Passive Women's Roles in a Newfoundland Fishery.' In J.N. Klein and D.L. Davis, eds. *To Work and To Weep: Women in Fishing Economies*. St John's: Institute of Social and Economic Research, Memorial University of Newfoundland.

Davis, Anthony. 1991. 'Insidious Rationalities: The Institutionalisation of Small Boat Fishing and the Rise of the Rapacious Fisher.' *MAST*: Maritime Anthropological Studies 4:1. 13–31.

Department of Rural, Agricultural and Northern Development. 1983. *Persistence and Change: The Social and Economic Development of Rural Newfoundland and Labrador, 1971 to 1981.* Research and Analysis Division. St John's: Government of Newfoundland and Labrador.

Dinham, Paul. 1977. *You Never Know What They Might Do.* St John's: Institute of Social and Economic Research, Memorial University of Newfoundland.

Economic Council of Canada. 1980. *Newfoundland: From Dependency to Self-Reliance.* Ottawa: Ministry of Supply and Services.

Elliot, R.M. 1980. 'Newfoundland Politics in the 1920's: The Genesis and Significance of the Hollis-Walker Inquiry.' In J.K. Hiller and Peter Neary, eds. *Newfoundland in the Nineteenth and Twentieth Centuries: Essays in Interpretation.* Toronto: University of Toronto Press. 181–204.

Ericson, Richard V. 1982. *Reproducing Order: A Study of Police Patrol Work.* Toronto: University of Toronto Press.

Fairley, Bryant. 1990. 'The Crisis, the State and Class Formation in the Newfoundland Fishery." In Fairley et al., eds. *Restructuring and Resistance: Perspectives from Atlantic Canada.* Toronto: Garamond Press. 171–202.

Fairley, Bryant, Colin Leys, and James Sacouman. 1990. *Restructuring and Resistance: Perspectives from Atlantic Canada.* Toronto: Garamond Press.

Faris, James C. 1973. *Cat Harbour: A Newfoundland Fishing Settlement.* St John's: Institute of Social and Economic Research, Memorial University of Newfoundland.

Felt, Larry. 1987. '"Take the 'Bloods of Bitches' to the Gallows": Cultural and Structural Constraints upon Interpersonal Violence in Rural Newfoundland.' ISER Research and Policy Paper no. 6. St John's: Institute of Social and Economic Research, Memorial University of Newfoundland.

Felt, Larry, and Peter Sinclair. 1990. 'Home Sweet Home! Dimensions and Determinants of Life Satisfaction in an Underdeveloped Region.' Paper presented at the Twenty-fifth Annual Meetings of the Atlantic Association of Sociologists and Anthropologists, Saint John, N.B.

Felt, Lawrence F., and Peter R. Sinclair. 1995a. 'Introduction.' Chapter 1 in Lawrence F. Felt and Peter R. Sinclair, eds. *Living on the Edge: The Great Northern Peninsula of Newfoundland.* St John's: Institute of Social and Economic Research, Memorial University of Newfoundland.

– 1995b. 'Conclusion.' Chapter 10 in Lawrence F. Felt and Peter R. Sinclair, eds. *Living on the Edge: The Great Northern Peninsula of Newfoundland.* St John's: Institute of Social and Economic Research, Memorial University of Newfoundland.

Felt, Lawrence, F., Kathleen Murphy, and Peter R. Sinclair. 1995a. 'Home Sweet Home: Dimensions and Determinants of Life Satisfaction.' Chapter 2 in Lawrence F. Felt and Peter R. Sinclair, eds. *Living on the Edge: The Great*

Northern Peninsula of Newfoundland. St John's: Institute of Social and Economic Research, Memorial University of Newfoundland.

– 1995b. '"Everyone Does It": Unpaid Work and Household Reproduction.' Chapter 4 in Lawrence F. Felt and Peter R. Sinclair, eds. *Living on the Edge: The Great Northern Peninsula of Newfoundland.* St John's: Institute of Social and Economic Research, Memorial University of Newfoundland.

Firestone, Melvin M. 1967. *Brothers and Rivals: Patrilocality in Savage Cove.* St John's: Institute of Social and Economic Research, Memorial University of Newfoundland.

– 1978. 'Socialization and Interaction in a Newfoundland Outport.' *Urban Life* 7:1 (April).

Fitzgerald, Jack. 1987. *Rogues and Branding Irons.* St John's: Jesperson Press.

Fleming, Thomas, ed. 1985. *The New Criminologies in Canada: State, Crime and Control.* Toronto: Oxford University Press.

Gartner, Rosemary, and Anthony N. Doob. 1996. 'Trends in Criminal Victimization: 1988–1993.' In R.A. Silverman, J.J. Teevan, and V.F. Sacco, eds. *Crime in Canadian Society.* 5th edition. Toronto: Harcourt Brace.

Gmelch, George, and Barnett Richling. 1988. '"We're Better Off Here": Return Migration to Newfoundland Outports.' *Anthropology Today* 4:4. 12–14.

Grady, Donald J., and R.J. Sacouman. 1990. '"Piracy," the Capitalist State and Proactive Struggle: The Woods Harbour Experience.' In Roxana Ng, G. Walker, and J. Muller, eds. *Community Organization and the Canadian State.* Toronto: Garamond Press.

Griffiths, Curt, J. Klein, and S. Verdun-Jones. 1980. *Criminal Justice in Canada.* Toronto: Butterworths.

Griffiths, Curt, and S. Verdun-Jones. 1994. *Canadian Criminal Justice.* 2nd edition. Toronto: Harcourt Brace.

Gunness, Margret. 1973. 'A Northeast Coast Community – A Spatial Analysis.' MA Thesis, Department of Anthropology, Memorial University of Newfoundland.

Gwyn, Richard. 1972. *Smallwood: The Unlikely Revolutionary.* Toronto: McClelland and Stewart.

Hagan, John. 1984. *The Disreputable Pleasures: Crime and Deviance in Canada.* 2nd edition. Toronto: McGraw-Hill Ryerson.

Hagedorn, Robert, ed. 1994. *Sociology.* 5th edition. Toronto: HBJ-Holt.

Hardin, Garrett. 1968. 'The Tragedy of the Commons.' *Science* 162. 1243–8.

Hewitt, Veronica. 1978. 'Growing Up in the Outports.' Undergraduate paper submitted to Folklore 2000. Memorial University of Newfoundland Folklore and Langauge Archive, accession no. 78–338.

Hinds, Lennox O'Reilly. 1995. 'Crisis in Canada's Atlantic Sea Fisheries.' *Marine Policy* 19:4. 271–83.

Horwood, Harold. 1968. *A History of the Newfoundland Ranger Force*. St John's: Breakwater Books.

House, J.D., S. White, and P. Ripley. 1989. *Going Away ... and Coming Back: Economic Life and Migration in Small Canadian Communities*. St John's: Institute of Social and Economic Research, Memorial University of Newfoundland.

Jackson, F.L. 1990. 'The Marxist Mystification of Newfoundland History.' *Newfoundland Studies* 6:2. 267–81.

Kaill, Robert C., and Paul Smith. 1984. *Atlantic Crime Profile*. Occasional Paper No. 1. Halifax: Atlantic Institute of Criminology, Dalhousie University.

Kennedy, L.W., and D.G. Dutton. 1989. 'The Incidence of Wife Assault in Alberta.' *Canadian Journal of Behavioral Science* 21. 40–54.

Klein, John F., J.R. Webb, and J.E. DiSanto. 1978. 'Experience with the Police and Attitude toward the Police.' *Canadian Journal of Sociology* 3:4. 441–56.

Koenig, Dan J. 1974. 'Correlates of Self-Reported Victimization and Perceptions of Neighbourhood Safety.' Mimeograph. Victoria: Department of Sociology, University of Victoria.

– 1987. 'Conventional Crime.' Chapter 12 in Rick Linden, ed. *Criminology: A Canadian Perspective*. 2nd edition. Toronto: Holt, Rinehart and Winston.

Laub, John H. 1981. 'Ecological Considerations in Victim Reporting to the Police.' *Journal of Criminal Justice* 9. 419–30.

– 1983. 'Patterns of Offending in Urban and Rural Areas.' *Journal of Criminal Justice* 11. 129–42.

Lortie, Dan. 1975. *Schoolteacher: A Sociological Study*. Chicago: University of Chicago Press.

Lyerly, Richard R., and J.K. Skipper. 1981. 'Differential Rates of Rural-Urban Delinquency: A Social Control Approach.' *Criminology* 19:3. 385–99.

Maclean's. 1993. 'Newfoundland: Can the Province Be Saved? Cover/Special Report, 23 August 1993. 19–28

Mandville, Doris M. 1974. 'Cyril Mandville: Moose Hunting on the Avalon Peninsula of Newfoundland.' Undergraduate paper submitted to Folklore 3400. Memorial University of Newfoundland Folklore and Language Archive, accession no. 75–36.

Martin, Cabot. 1990. 'Comment on Sinclair's "Fisheries Management and Problems of Social Justice: Reflections on the Northwest Coast of Newfoundland."' *MAST: Maritime Anthropological Studies* 2:2. 103–10.

Matthews, Ralph. 1975. *There's No Better Place Than Here: Social Change in Three Newfoundland Communities*. Toronto: Peter Martin Associates.

Matthews, Ralph, and John Phyne. 1988. 'Regulating the Newfoundland Inshore Fishery: Traditional Values Versus State Control in the Regulation of a Common Property Resource.' *Journal of Canadian Studies* 23:1&2. 158–76.

McDonald, Ian. 1980. 'W.F. Coaker and the Balance of Power Strategy: The Fisherman's Protective Union in Newfoundland Politics.' In J.K. Hiller and Peter Neary, eds. *Newfoundland in the Nineteenth and Twentieth Centuries: Essays in Interpretation.* Toronto: University of Toronto Press. 148–80.

McGrath, Darrin. n.d. #1 'Poaching in Newfoundland and Labrador: The Creation of an Issue.' Unpublished MA paper. Department of Sociology, Memorial University of Newfoundland.

– n.d. #2. 'Poaching in Contemporary Newfoundland: An Ethnographic Account.' Unpublished MA paper. Department of Sociology, Memorial University of Newfoundland.

– 1992. 'Poaching in Newfoundland and Labrador: The Creation of an Issue.' Thesis submitted to the School of Graduate Studies in partial fulfilment of the requirements for the degree of Master of Arts. Department of Sociology, Memorial University of Newfoundland.

–1994. 'Salted Caribou and Sportsmen-Tourists: Conflicts over Wildlife Resources in Newfoundland at the Turn of the Twentieth Century.' *Newfoundland Studies* 10:2. 208–25.

McGrath, W.T., and M.P. Mitchell. 1981. *The Police Function in Canada.* Toronto: Methuen.

McMullan, John, D.C. Perrier, and N.R. Okihiro. 1988. 'Law, Regulation and Illegality in the Nova Scotia Lobster Fishery.' Occasional Papers Series. Halifax: Atlantic Institute of Criminology, Dalhousie University.

Meltzer, Evelyn. 1994. 'Global Overview of Straddling and Highly Migratory Fish Stocks: The Nonsustainable Nature of High Seas Fisheries.' *Ocean Development and International Law* 25. 255–344.

Mercer, W.E., and F. Manuel. 1974. 'Some Aspects of Moose Management in Newfoundland.' *Naturaliste Canadien* 101. 657–71.

Mills, C. Wright. 1959. *The Sociological Imagination.* Toronto: Oxford University Press.

Murphy, Kathleen. 1995. 'Maternal Politics: Women's Political Struggles in a Logging Town.' Chapter 8 in Lawrence F. Felt and Peter R. Sinclair, eds. *Living on the Edge: The Great Northern Peninsula of Newfoundland.* St John's: Institute of Social and Economic Research, Memorial University of Newfoundland.

Neary, Peter. 1980. 'Party Politics in Newfoundland 1949–1971: A Survey and Analysis.' In J.K. Hiller and Peter Neary, eds. *Newfoundland in the Nineteenth and Twentieth Centuries: Essays in Interpretation.* Toronto: University of Toronto Press. 205–45.

Neis, Barbara. 1991. 'Flexible Specialization: What's That Got to Do with the Price of Fish?' *Studies in Political Economy* 36 (Fall). 145–75.
– 1993. 'From "Shipped Girls" to "Brides of the State": The Transition from Familial to Social Patriarchy in the Newfoundland Fishing Industry.' *Canadian Journal of Regional Science* 16:2. 185–211.
Newfoundland and Labrador. 1982. *The Wild Life Act: Revised Statutes of Newfoundland.* St John's: Government of Newfoundland and Labrador.
Newfoundland and Labrador Hydro. 1980. 'Socio-Economic Impact Study of the Proposed Northeast Coast Hydroelectric Project.' Final Report prepared by Saga Developments/Omnifacts Research for Newfoundland and Labrador Hydro.
Newfoundland and Labrador Wildlife Division. 1985. *Green Paper on Hunting.* St John's: Government of Newfoundland and Labrador.
– 1986–7. *Hunting Guide.* St John's: Government of Newfoundland and Labrador.
Newfoundland Colonial Secretary's Office. 1923. *Census of Newfoundland and Labrador, 1921.* St John's: Colonial Secretary's Office.
Newfoundland Department of Rural, Agricultural and Northern Development. 1983. Persistence and Change: The Social and Economic Development of Rural Newfoundland and Labrador, 1971 to 1981. St John's: Research and Analysis Division.
Newman, Peter C. 1994. 'To Kill a People – Dash Their Dream.' *Maclean's*, 25 April. 45.
O'Grady, Bill. 1986. 'Popular Anxiety and Violence in Newfoundland.' Paper presented at the Atlantic Association of Sociologists and Anthropologists Annual Meetings, Acadia University, Wolfville, N.S.
– 1989. 'Crime, Violence and Victimization: A Newfoundland Case.' *Canadian Criminology Forum* 10. 1–15.
O'Neill, Paul. 1976. *A Seaport Legacy: The Story of St. John's, Newfoundland.* Erin, Ont.: Press Porcepic.
Omohundro, John T. 1993. *Rough Food: The Seasons of Subsistence in Northern Newfoundland.* Social and Economic Studies no. 54. St John's: Institute of Social and Economic Research, Memorial University of Newfoundland.
Overton, James. 1980. 'Tourism Development, Conservation and Conflict: Game Laws for Caribou Protection in Newfoundland.' Source: Memorial University of Newfoundland.
– 1990. 'A Critical Look at Responses to the Problem of Youth Unemployment in Newfoundland.' In Janet Burns and Chris McCormick, eds. *From the Margin to the Center: Proceedings of the 25th Anniversary Meetings of the Atlantic Association of Sociologists and Anthropologists.* Saint John: University of New Brunswick.

Palmer, Craig T. 1995a. 'The Troubled Fishery: Conflicts, Decisions and Fishery Policy.' Chapter 3 in Lawrence F. Felt and Peter R. Sinclair, eds. *Living on the Edge: The Great Northern Peninsula of Newfoundland.* St John's: Institute of Social and Economic Research, Memorial University of Newfoundland.

– 1995b. 'Growing Female Roots in Patrilocal Soil: Cod Traps, Fish Plants and Changing Attitudes towards Women's Property Rights.' Chapter 7 in Lawrence F. Felt and Peter R. Sinclair eds. *Living on the Edge: The Great Northern Peninsula of Newfoundland.* St John's: Institute of Social and Economic Research, Memorial University of Newfoundland.

Perrier, David C. n.d., 'Professor on Patrol: An Academic's View of Policing as a Special Constable.' Department of Sociology, St Mary's University, Halifax, N.S.

Philbrook, Tom. 1966. *Fisherman, Logger, Merchant, Miner: Social Change and Industrialism in Three Newfoundland Communities.* St John's: Institute of Social and Economic Research, Memorial University of Newfoundland.

Phillips, G. Howard, and Todd N. Wurschmidt. 1982. 'The Ohio Rural Victimization Study.' In Timothy J. Carter, G.H. Phillips, J.F. Donnermeyer, and T.N. Wurschmidt, eds. *Rural Crime: Integrating Research and Prevention.* Totowa, N.J.: Allanheld, Osmun Publishers.

Phyne, John. 1990. 'Dispute Settlement in the Newfoundland Inshore Fishery.' *MAST: Maritime Anthropological Studies* 3:2 88–102.

Pollard, Eloyal. 1974. 'Dialect, Dialogue and Some Anecdotes of a Northeast Coast Community.' Undergraduate paper submitted to Folklore 3420. Memorial University of Newfoundland Folklore and Language Archive, accession no. 74–46.

Porter, M. 1982. '"A Tangly Bunch": The Political Culture of Outport Women in Newfoundland.' Unpublished paper.

– 1983. 'Women and Old Boats: The Sexual Division of Labour in a Newfoundland Outport.' In E. Garnikow, ed. *Public and Private: Gender and Society.* London: Heinemann.

Prowse, D.W. 1895. *A History of Newfoundland from the English, Colonial and Foreign Records.* London: Macmillan and Company.

Puddester, David. n.d. 'Outport Study – A Northeast Coast Community.' Paper prepared for History 3121. In Folklore and Language Archive, Memorial University of Newfoundland.

Quigley, Jean Marie. 1981. 'Moonshining in a Northeast Coast Community: Based on the Personal Experience of John Quigley.' Undergraduate paper submitted to English 3420. Memorial University of Newfoundland Folklore and Language Archive, accession no. 81–490.

Quinney, Richard. 1975. *Criminology: Analysis and Critique of Crime in America.* Toronto: Little, Brown and Company.

– 1979. *Criminology.* 2nd edition. Toronto: Little, Brown and Company.

Ratner, R.S. 1985. 'Inside the Liberal Boot: The Criminological Enterprise in Canada.' In T. Fleming, ed. *The New Criminologies in Canada: State, Crime and Control.* Toronto: Oxford University Press.

Richling, Barnett. 1985. '"You'd Never Starve Here": Return Migration to Rural Newfoundland.' *Canadian Review of Sociology and Anthropology* 22:2 236–49.

The Rounder. 1979. Gander: Newfoundland and Labrador Rural Development Council.

Royal Commission on Employment and Unemployment. 1986. *Building on Our Strengths.* St John's: Queen's Printer.

Ryan, Shannon. 1980. 'The Newfoundland Salt Cod Trade in the Nineteenth Century.' In J.K. Hiller and Peter Neary, eds. *Newfoundland in the Nineteenth and Twentieth Centuries: Essays in Interpretation.* Toronto: University of Toronto Press. 40–66.

Schrank, William E. 1995. 'Extended Fisheries Jurisdiction: Origins of the Current Crisis in Atlantic Canada's Fisheries.' *Marine Policy* 19:4. 285–9.

Schrank, William E., Noel Roy, Rosemary Ommer, and Blanca Skoda. 1992. 'An Inshore Fishery: A Commercially Viable Industry or an Employer of Last Resort.' *Ocean Development and International Law* 23. 335–67.

Schrank, William E., B. Skoda, N. Roy, and E. Tsoa. 1987. 'Canadian Government Financial Intervention in a Marine Fishery: The Case of Newfoundland, 1972/3–1980/1.' *Ocean Development and International Law* 18:2. 533–84.

Sider, Gerald. 1980. 'The Ties That Bind: Culture and Agriculture, Propriety and Property in the Newfoundland Village Fishery.' Draft paper in Centre for Newfoundland Studies, Memorial University of Newfoundland.

– 1982. 'Family Fun in Starve Harbour: Custom, History and Confrontation in Village Newfoundland.' Paper in Centre for Newfoundland Studies, Memorial University of Newfoundland.

– 1986. *Culture and Class in Anthropology and History.* London: Cambridge University Press.

Sinclair, Peter. 1990. 'Fisheries Management and Problems of Social Justice: Reflections on Northwest Newfoundland.' *MAST: Maritime Anthropological Studies* 3:1. 30–47.

Sinclair, Peter R., and Lawrence F. Felt. 1993. 'Coming Back: Return Migration to Newfoundland's Great Northern Peninsula.' *Newfoundland Studies* 9:1. 1–25.

Smallwood, Joseph, ed. 1981. *The Encyclopedia of Newfoundland and Labrador.* St John's: Newfoundland Book Publishers.

Smith, Brent L., and C.R. Huff. 1982. 'Crime in the Country: The Vulnerability and Victimization of Rural Citizens.' *Journal of Criminal Justice* 10. 271–82.

Solicitor-General of Canada. 1983. 'Victims of Crime.' Canadian Urban Victimization Survey. Ottawa: Solicitor-General of Canada.

– 1984. 'Reported and Unreported Crimes.' Canadian Urban Victimization Survey. Ottawa: Solicitor General of Canada.

Sparkes, R.F. 1983. *The Winds Softly Sigh*. 2nd edition. St John's: Breakwater Books.

Statistics Canada. 1986. *Policing in Canada 1986*. Canadian Centre for Justice Statistics, Catalogue 85-523.

Stebbins, Robert A. 1971. *Commitment to Deviance: The Nonprofessional Criminal in the Community*. Westport, Conn.: Greenwood Publishing Corporation.

Story, G.M., W.J. Kirwin, and J.D.A. Widdowson. 1982. *Dictionary of Newfoundland English*. Toronto: University of Toronto Press.

– 1990. *Dictionary of Newfoundland English*. 2nd edition. Toronto: University of Toronto Press.

Szala, Karen. 1978. '"Clean Women and Quiet Men": Courtship and Marriage in a Newfoundland Fishing Village.' Thesis submitted in partial fulfilment of the requirements for the degree of Master of Arts. Department of Anthropology, Memorial University of Newfoundland.

Szwed, John. 1966: *Private Cultures and Public Imagery: Interpersonal Relations in a Newfoundland Peasant Society*. St John's: Institute of Social and Economic Research, Memorial University of Newfoundland.

Task Force on Incomes and Adjustment in the Atlantic Fishery. 1993. *Charting a New Course: Towards the Fishery of the Future*. Ottawa: Communications Directorate, Department of Fisheries and Oceans.

Taylor, Ian, Paul Walton, and Jock Young. 1973. *The New Criminology: For a Social Theory of Deviance*. London: Routledge and Kegan Paul.

Teevan, James J., ed. 1992. *Introduction to Sociology: A Canadian Focus*. 4th edition. Scarborough, Ont. Prentice-Hall Canada.

Thomas, Richard H. 1983. *The Politics of Hunting*. Aldershot, Hants: Gower Publishing.

Thompson, Edward P. 1975. *Whigs and Hunters: The Origin of the Black Act*. London: Allen Lane.

Wadel, Cato. 1986. *Now, Whose Fault Is That?: The Struggle for Self-Esteem in the Face of Chronic Unemployment*. Newfoundland Social and Economic Studies no. 11. St John's: Institute of Social and Economic Research, Memorial University of Newfoundland.

Waller, Irvin, and Norman Okihiro. 1978. *Burglary: The Victim and the Public*. Toronto: University of Toronto Press.

Walsh, Shannon. 1991. 'Newfoundland's South Coast Smuggling Operation.' Unpublished paper prepared for Sociology 332. Department of Sociology, Mount Saint Vincent University.

Warner, John R. 1978. *Rural Crime: A Bibliography.* Monticello, Ill.: Vance Bibliographies.

Welbourn, Kathryn. 1995. 'Outport and Outlaws.' *Equinox* 83 (September/October). 34–43.

Widdowson, John. 1977. *If You Don't Be Good: Verbal Social Control in Newfoundland.* St John's: Institute of Social and Economic Research, Memorial University of Newfoundland.

Wildlife Management Institute. 1955. *The Wildlife of Newfoundland.* A Report by the Wildlife Management Institute, Washington, D.C. St John's: Ministry of Mines and Resources.

Wiley, Mary Glenn, and Terry L. Hudik. 1974. 'Police-Citizen Encounters: A Field Test of Exchange Theory.' *Social Problems* 22. 119–26.

Williams, Rick, with Gilles Theriault. 1990. 'Crisis and Response: Underdevelopment in the Fishery and the Evolution of the Maritime Fishermen's Union.' In R.J. Brym and R.J. Sacouman, eds. *Underdevelopment and Social Movements in Atlantic Canada.* Toronto: New Hogtown Press.

Wilson, James Q. 1968. *Varieties of Police Behaviour.* Cambridge, Mass.: Harvard University Press.

Index